W9-BRC-442

PIMPS UP, HO'S DOWN

Pimps Up, Ho's Down

HIP HOP'S HOLD ON YOUNG BLACK WOMEN

T. DENEAN SHARPLEY-WHITING

NEW YORK UNIVERSITY PRESS

NEW YORK AND LONDON

NEW YORK UNIVERSITY PRESS
New York and London
www.nyupress.org

© 2007 by New York University

Library of Congress Cataloging-in-Publication Data
Sharpley-Whiting, T. Denean.
Pimps up, ho's down : hip hop's hold on young Black women /
Tracy D. Sharpley-Whiting.
p. cm.
Includes bibliographical references and index.
ISBN-13: 978-0-8147-4014-9 (cloth : alk. paper)
ISBN-10: 0-8147-4014-6 (cloth : alk. paper)
1. African American women—Social conditions. 2. Young women—United
States—Social conditions. 3. Hip-hop—Social aspects—United States.
4. Sex role—Political aspects—United States. 5. Sexism—United States.
6. African American women—Psychology. 7. Young women—United
States—Psychology. 8. African American women—Interviews. 9. Young
women—United States—Interviews. 10. United States—
Social conditions—1980– I. Title.
E185.86.S515 2007
305.48'896073—dc22 2006101234

New York University Press books are printed on acid-free paper,
and their binding materials are chosen for strength and durability.

Manufactured in the United States of America
10 9 8 7 6 5 4 3

CONTENTS

ACKNOWLEDGMENTS

here are many people who
have assisted me in writing this book. There were times
when I had just had enough and those individuals offered
support, encouragement, and feedback. I would like to
thank my editor, Eric Zinner, Emily Park, as well as the production and marketing team at NYU Press. Your enthusiasm
at the early stages was catching. I would like to thank my
former colleagues at Hamilton College and those at Vanderbilt University, in particular Mona Frederick at the Robert
Penn Warren Center for the Humanities, Linda Manning,
Director of the Women's Center, and Monica Casper, Director of Women's and Gender Studies. Thanks to Aishah Simmons (everyone should view NO!:therapedocumentary.com),
Nekesa Moody, whose essay on hip hop and women continues to be inspiring, and Elizabeth Hadley. Ketura D. Brown,
my research assistant, deserves a special thanks for her dedi-
cation and smarts. I'd also like to thank Alice Randall (keep
those novels coming), Tiffany Patterson, Thadious Davis,
W. Jelani Cobb, Davarian Baldwin, Yelitza Nieves, Pamela
Des Barres, rock and roll's first groupie to tell all, Tiona Mc-
Clodden, Dwight McBride, and Mireille Miller-Young for
the intriguing conversation on net porn in Brazil at ASWAD.
I'd like to thank the Frist Center for Visual Arts in Nash-

ville, where I volunteer twice a month, for providing a space
for contemplation in the Art Library, Mark Anthony Neal,
Marcyliena Morgan and the Hip Hop Archive at Stanford
University, Joy James, Julie Beverly, editor and publisher of
Ozone magazine, Jonathan Shecter of Game Video, Inc., the
young women interviewees in the book's concluding chapter
as well as Anna and the women in various strip clubs who
shared their experiences, Michael Eric Dyson and Reverend
Marcia Dyson, and Darlene Clark-Hine, who listened to me
express misgivings one morning at the Hilton Garden Inn in
Evanston, IL; and last but certainly not least, hip hop and
feminism—may we continue the dialogue.

I have to thank my extended family as well as my parents,
Muriel and Gina Sharpley. Gilman Whiting, thank you for
your wit and proofreading; and Haviland, thank you for pa-
tiently drawing pictures of princesses and queens and singing
wonderful songs as Mommy typed.

PROLOGUE

Sex, Power, and Punanny

So listen up all the ladies, nubian queens,
black princesses, african goddesses, choir girls,
    young girls, models,
skeezas, bitches, hos, playettes, dykes, divas,
    house wives, gold diggers,
sac chasers, cum guzzlers, chicken heads, crack
    heads, baller bitches,
shake dancers and boosters.
Say what you want, we're all one in the same.
No matter what they call you, or you call your-
    self.
There's only 3 rules in this game:
keep your nappy-ass hair done, do your mother
    fucking sit-ups,
and whenever you lay on your back, make sure
    your paper is stacked.
        —"INTRO" BY SOMMORE, Trina's *Diamond*
        Princess

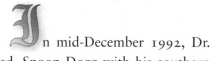n mid-December 1992, Dr.
Dre's *The Chronic* dropped. Snoop Dogg with his southern
drawl reminded me of home—St. Louis—before names like
Nellyville and The Lou caught on. St. Louis has a markedly
southern-derived black culture thanks to the black migration
from the rural South to cities up north in search of better
lives and jobs. My maternal side of the family was living

proof of that migration: they were formerly tenant farmers on a plantation in Aberdeen, Mississippi. However, raised by my ambitious single black father with the help of his practical midwestern mother and grandmother, I only heard those southern inflections in the neighborhood alleyways where I played kickball and "cork"—tomboy that I was—with other kids, or when visiting my mother's family.

Though my father speaks in that highly sought-after news-anchor-style regional-accent-free diction, by the time I reached college in the Northeast, several friends called me "Twang." Words like hair, chair, and care came out flat and with a "u" where the "ai" should have been and double "r's" replaced words ending in "re": *churr, hurr, curr.* Over the years I had worked to shed the accent as I continued my education in the Northeast (though it still naturally reasserts itself in the company of those closest to me). But as I strolled into the Rites and Reasons Theatre one Tuesday morning in March 1993, I was doing my best impression of Snoop's "One, two, three and to the fo' " from "Nuthin' But a G-Thang."

I was one of three graduate teaching assistants for Professor Michael Eric Dyson's Introduction to African American Studies class at Brown University and it was my day to lecture before the class of sixty plus students. We were reading and discussing bell hooks's provocative essay "Selling Hot Pussy: Representations of Black Female Sexuality in the Cultural Marketplace." It was one of those rare moments where my contradictions were laid bare—humming such a salacious, sexist tune after immersing myself in the brilliance of hooks. But of course, that (and my accent-repressing acrobatics) was just the beginning of my contradictions.

Perhaps I was too implicated in the essay. hooks's bit about modeling sent me into a tailspin. In my lecture, I waxed on about the modeling profession—explaining the strides black models had made and commenting on the continued color and size biases of the industry as well as the practice of calling women "girls." The students were chomping at the bit. Phrases such as "oppressive beauty standards," "anorexia," and "bulimia," came rushing toward me at the podium. The Brown undergraduates were sharp. This was the era before the popularity of Tyra Banks's *America's Next Top Model,* the height of Naomi Wolf's exciting *The Beauty Myth,* and so the debate began. Dyson sat bemused in the audience, listening. The quick-witted womanist thinker Marcia Dyson was also there. Together we engaged the students in a lively back and forth on beauty culture, black women, and their own refusal to undertake that same rigorous critique of sexism in rap music and videos. Who was I to talk about "rigorous critique"? I slinked out of the classroom at noon and hopped into my car with *The Chronic* blasting. I was on my way to Boston to model in a mid-afternoon runway show at Saks Fifth Avenue.

In hindsight, I realize that models, like the strip club dancers and "video vixens" (disparagingly referred to as "video-ho's") that I discuss in this book, and even female rappers such as Trina, Lil' Kim, and Foxy Brown, occupy a peculiar place of cultural antipathy. We are all in the business of selling illusions, as we move various products—including our own sexuality—but we often stand accused of selling out. Blamed for participating in the exploitation of women, these women and their stories, like mine, are always much more complicated. Nothing—be it modeling, stripping, or rapping about punanny power, and the motivations behind such choices—is ever so clear cut.

My turn as a print and runway model primarily involved a desire to live above the poverty line as a graduate student. While the four-year Dorothy Danforth Compton fellowship at Brown was generous, the monthly stipend was wanting. I had won out on some counts in the genetic roll of the die, and so modeling seemed a viable alternative.

Like erotic dancers, I assumed the money would be fast and easy. Like my fellow Brown alum Heidi Mattson, whose book *Ivy League Stripper* describes her tenure at Brown as a student by day, Providence Foxy Lady stripper by night (or dayshift), I did not necessarily see modeling as conspiring with the multibillion-dollar beauty and sex entertainment industries. Many of my graduate student colleagues found my choice of pick-up work anti-intellectual. Some even attributed my success in graduate school to high heels, long legs, and short skirts. I, on the other hand, had come to fully appreciate the meaning of the Ph.D.—Player Hating Degree.

With my feet in both worlds, I felt quite grounded. When I overheard models obsess about their imperfections, breast jobs, "go-sees" (castings), photographers, and comp cards, I envisioned a career as an intellectual. When my academic colleagues took themselves way too seriously, I turned to the less-lofty world of modeling. It is not that models are stick-figured pinheads; they just don't get worked up about Hegelian dialectics. If an academic job didn't materialize, I informed my dissertation advisor that I would return to Paris (I had an agency—Specimen) to work on my "book" (modeling portfolio) and seriously pursue modeling, instead of tracking down obscure documents in the libraries and archives of the Bibliothèque Nationale de France and the Musée de l'Homme.

It was the perfect mind-body split. Like Kimberly Jones, who professes in a 2000 interview in *The Washington Post* with Kristal Brent Zook that "Lil' Kim is what I use to get money . . . a character I use to sell my records," I too was whatever the client, photographer, or my agent wanted me to be—lingerie runway model, African American girl next door, high-fashion print model. I didn't anticipate the hours on the Stairmaster and the verbal blows delivered with precision to the body or face by an agent, photographer, client, or even a make-up artist. I remember doing a freebie runway show for the high-end salon Safar on Newberry Street in Boston, which netted me a year and a half of cuts, coloring, and styling by a skillful Czechoslovakian stylist. When I sat in the make-up artist's chair with my hair teased about wildly, he frowned but went to work. Afterwards, he remarked how fabulous I looked; he had wondered what was so special when I first sat down. And he was so sincere. These were also pre-Beyoncé and Jennifer Lopez days. And my hankerings for sweet potato pie, hot chocolate, and peach cobbler easily moved my 5'10", 118 lb. frame from a size six to an eight—plus-size model territory.

Despite the hoo-hah in the Brown classroom that day, I was a card-carrying member of the Rhode Island chapter of NOW (National Organization for Women). My progressive politics were unwavering. They had been shaped by uncles who flirted with Marxist-Humanism and "Free Angela Davis" campaigns and parents who gnashed their teeth about Reaganomics. In the mid- to late 1980s, I had plunged into four years of intense study and dialogue on race, sex, gender, class, and politics at an elite, private coeducational university in upstate New York. I found Paula Giddings's *When I and Where I Enter* inspiring and Barbara Smith's *All the Women Are White, All the Men Are Black, But Some of Us Are Brave: Black Women's Studies* all that and then some. My first encounter with Gloria Watkins (bell hooks) was at a forum sponsored by a multiracial women's student organization that myself and another student co-founded. With her seeming affection for titles with the word "pussy" in them, she discussed her essay "Whose Pussy Is It?"—a critique of Spike Lee's *She's Gotta Have It,* black sexual politics, and feminism. Belatedly recognizing that unforgettable scene between Nola Darling and her paramour, Jamie Overstreet, as one of rape, Spike Lee now wishes that it had been left on the cutting room floor. In a 1998 interview, "[He Got] Game Plan," with Gary Dauphin of *The Village Voice,* Lee reflects on his breakout film:

> I would take the rape scene out of *She's Gotta Have It.* . . . Rape is obviously a very violent act, and I just wish I hadn't put the scene in. It brought a lot of things into the picture that didn't belong there, and it just wasn't necessary. It was my ignorance at the time that I put it there. . . . [N]obody TOLD me. I'm 41 now. I was 24 when I wrote that script. It just didn't belong in the movie. You grow and you learn.

We had all seen Lee's film when it debuted, stunned into silence by the "whose pussy is it" scene. And yet, we were not quite audacious enough to muster the word "rape"—though rape it was.

We were students galvanized by apartheid, steeped in rap music, and committed to extracurricular reading groups, black studies courses, and faculty-supervised independent study on black women's literature and history, so much so that by the time I reached Brown University as a graduate student, French feminist theory had had its shot at me and black women's studies were squarely on my radar, with hip hop always somewhere blaring in the background. We were part of a new black youth culture, "the hip hop generation" as MBA Wharton school graduate Ivan Juzang first put it in a 1992 market-research piece released by Motivational Educational Entertainment, "Reaching the Hip-Hop Generation." This term defines those born in the post-movement era—post–civil rights, black power, and women's movements—yet profoundly influenced by those movements. It is a term that transcends geography in that it refers to those coming from urban epicenters and suburban outposts. And in the context of this book, it refers specifically to blacks born between approximately 1965 and 1984.[1]

Despite my fellowship with hip hop, the relationship between young women and hip hop, even in those late 1980s college days, proved knotty in places. When the late Scott La Rock had "had 'em all" being a "super ho" with his "super sperm," I often wondered just how many "fly girls, shy girls, black girls, white girls" he had run up in and then kicked to the curb. An undeniably unflattering depiction of male boarishness, La Rock's reference to himself as a "super ho" nonetheless reflected the universal use of the term "ho," quite unlike its exclusive use for women in post-1980s hip hop.

Even Sir Mix A Lot's booty anthems, a precursor to 2 Live Crew, and the friendly fire battles of "Roxanne, Roxanne," Roxanne Shante, and "The Real Roxanne," left us all standing intact. The seemingly endless parade of Roxannes—part of the first wave of female rappers—Salt-N-Pepa, MC Lyte, Latifah, and Monie Love (the second wave), presented young women with an alternative worldview, a female perspective on the underclass, urban youth, and sexual politics. However, these progressive counterpoints were often overshadowed by women's footnoted status in hip hop.

As the grind and ravages of the Reagan-Bush eras whirred along thrashing urban communities, youth unemployment rose unchecked along with crack-cocaine addiction, and dealing became a full-time job. Gangsta rap emerged to hold it down for the West Coast and the South with Scarface and others. That genre of rap music provided insights similar to Grandmaster Flash and the Furious Five's "The Message," as it described the depressed and violent environs of the mostly black and Latino Los Angeles and the Deep South, but it was a mixed one as far as gender. The war on drugs led to prison culture and black youth culture meeting somewhere in the middle. Scores of black and brown men, fresh from juvenile detention centers or prison stints, defined a new masculinity in which the unique sexual hierarchies formed in those spaces were transferred to heterosexual relations. Outside these institutional walls, women became the proverbial "punks in prisons"—those incarcerated men described as "bitches" and "ho's," used to satisfy sexual needs, tasked with prison clean-up, cooking, laundry duties, etc., and oftentimes exploited brutally to assert manhood and masculinity.

From the late 1980s onwards, the gender-bending term "ho" was exclusively used to describe women or "unmanly" men, and "bitch" could be heard ad nauseam. The "g's up, ho's down" mentality of late 1980s hip hop laid the groundwork for the "pimp-playa-bitch-ho" nexus that has come to dominate hip hop culture. A third wave of stalwart female rappers—Lauryn Hill, Missy Elliot, Eve—emerged that nonetheless also included artists who many accused of pandering to the nexus, thus representing a marked departure from first- and second-wave female hip hop artists. For some, this pandering ran parallel to a new wave in feminism of the sex-power-punanny variety. Lil' Kim, Shawnna, Jacki-O, Remy Ma, Trina, and Foxy Brown were pushing the envelope with respect to gender relations, sexuality, and beauty culture. Alternately called "feminist glamazons" or rainmakers of a "new" or "post" feminist era (seems folks can't make up their minds whether feminism is indeed passé), they fearlessly exemplified punanny politics, status consumption, and the ever-provocative word "bitch." And so while this bitchy hip hop sextuplet rapped about sex as part of a young woman's arsenal to be deployed when necessary (and definitely for money), and frequently reclined at the altar of beauty culture as enabling rather than oppressive, their more egg-headed counterparts founded the magazine *Bitch: Feminist Response to Pop Culture* in 1996.

While the editors of *Bitch* surprisingly tiptoe around the issue of hip hop and the "bitchy sextuplet," their pitch regarding the magazine's name rings a strikingly familiar tone. In the same way that hip hop embraced and redefined the "n-word," the magazine's mission statement suggests that "bitch" describes "all at once who we are when we speak up, what it is we're too worked up over to be quiet about, and the act of making ourselves heard."

Though *Bitch* "refuses to ignore the contradictory and sometimes uncomfortable details that constitute the realities of women's lives," I don't think the "Queen Bee" Lil' Kim (who identifies herself as a feminist), "Da Baddest Bitch" Trina, or "That Beeyatch" Remy Ma will be gracing the magazine's covers or interiors anytime soon. Perhaps those "bitches'" contradictions are too uncomfortable and raw for *Bitch*; but what their exclusion aptly points to is the fork in the road between hip hop and feminism—mainstream, black, or otherwise.

It is in this in-between space where I would like to dwell. I believe we have reached a fascinating, and predictably retrogressive, moment in American pop culture regarding class, gender, and race. As a member of the hip hop generation, I am continually intrigued by the ways in which hip hop sets the tone for how women—myself included—think and act. I have written this book as a way to explore how and why we women do the things we do, what hip hop has to say about it all, and what we have to say back.

INTRODUCTION

Pimpin' Ain't Easy, But Somebody's Got to Do It

This is a man's world
But it wouldn't be nothing without a woman or
a girl.
— JAMES BROWN, "It's a Man's, Man's World"

Women are the weaker sex. . . . women's bodies
are made to attract and to please men. . . . now
that women are equal, they should be able to ac-
cept being told that they aren't, quite.
— HARVEY MANSFIELD, *Manliness*

When hip hop impresario
Russell Simmons appeared at Hamilton College for an evening lecture on "Hip Hop, Culture, and Politics" in April
2004, no one could have anticipated the fallout. Simmons,
considered a veritable maverick in the hip hop industry, co-
founded with Rick Rubin the highly successful record label
Def Jam. Under Def Jam, Simmons promoted and developed
rap acts like Kurtis Blow, LL Cool J, and the first crossover
rap triumvirate, Run DMC, in which his brother Joseph
Simmons—the "Run" in the DMC—was also a member.

He would later go on to establish another label, Russell
Simmons Music Group. Setting up a quasi-entertainment and
fashion empire through his company Rush Communications,
Simmons's entrepreneurial talents expanded to include a

clothing company, Phat Farm, which was sold in 2004 to the tune of $140 million, soft drinks (DefCon3), television shows such as *Def Comedy Jam,* and a Broadway show with spoken word acts in *Def Poetry Jam. The New York Times* estimates that he sold his stake in Def Jam in 1999 for over $100 million to Universal Music Group. Indeed, his net worth hovers around $400 million. It is Simmons's power moves and business acumen that set the pace and tone for the likes of Shawn "Jay-Z" Carter and the more flamboyant Sean "Puffy" Combs.

But all these accomplishments were not the reason for his invitation to lecture at Hamilton College. Russell Simmons is also the chairman of the Hip Hop Summit Action Network (HSAN). The year 2004 was a critical election year for many who were tired of the mendacity and chicanery of the Bush administration. Some were also openly smarting from the voter fraud and widespread black disenfranchisement in Florida in 2000. Simmons's HSAN had voter registration among hip hop generationers and other political and social machinations as their mission, which included challenging the New York State Rockefeller drug laws as unethical, racially biased, and harshly punitive.

His lecture morphed into a Q&A session, as he made a last-minute decision to stray from the contractual script toward a "just kickin' it" dialogue. As with comedian Dave Chappelle's bodacious, street-cred-upholding character in the skit "When Keeping It Real Goes Wrong," Simmons's attempt at "keeping it real" fell flat. The result was a number of challenging questions from female audience members about hip hop culture, sex, and women.

Riled by the television show *BET Uncut,* and specifically the rapper Nelly's sexually provocative video "Tip Drill," female students swapped volleys with Simmons. At one point he dismissively chided the students about being up at 2 a.m.—apparently, the so-called godfather of hip hop had forgotten the crucial late-night aspect of the college experience. He went on further to suggest that the students just "turn off their television sets," an increasingly used line by corporate representatives when directly confronted by critics of such programming. Simmons's argument had the effect of identifying him more with his lucrative financial interests than with his audience. The students, of course, could have easily turned off their television sets. But they were more concerned about the millions of other television sets (79,999,998 to be exact, given BET's recent market penetration) that were left on, and the unpleasant gender politics and sexual provocations that continually flowed from them.[1]

One of the Hamilton students, a young woman, was especially agitated. While she was clearly misguided in her assertion that there were no networks devoted to promoting white culture (I sat mouth agape thinking about MTV, VH1, NBC, ABC, FOX, CBS, etc.), she nonetheless rightly zeroed in on hip hop culture's contradictory relationship with women, and boldly declared that these videos impinged upon her sense of womanhood. As she fled the auditorium in a huff, Simmons delivered the "keep it street" coup de grace. He attempted to evoke empathy for the hard-knock life of so many male rappers. He suggested that after acquiring the requisite material trappings of success—cars, houses, jewelry, and "all the pussy" they wanted—many rappers were still quite unfulfilled. I stifled a "What?" on the order of crunkmaster Lil' Jon. Audible gasps could be heard in the auditorium, almost filled to capacity. With the president and dean of the college and a gaggle of professors in the audience, Simmons's "When Keeping It Real Goes [Very] Wrong" moment exemplified for many the role that hip hop has carved out for young women. They were either "hot pussy for sale"—and hence Nelly swipes a credit card through a young woman's buttocks in the now infamous "Tip Drill" video—or they were "pussy for the taking," as Louisiana rapper Mystikal explains in "Pussy Crook."

But of course, hip hop's relationship to young women is much more complicated and varied than that. I also realize that hip hop, like every other socio-cultural and political phenomenon, has its quasi-saints and wholesale sinners. Some artists are just trying to make a buck; other hip hop artists can barely be called artists at all. But nevertheless, in the course of just my own lifetime, hip hop has risen from schoolyard battle sessions to become an astounding cultural force. Hip hop artists speak to, and for, a generation very often described as alienated and disaffected—feelings voiced by Kanye West, who blasted George W. Bush during the ongoing saga of Hurricane Katrina in New Orleans with those now-famous seven unscripted words: "George Bush doesn't care about black people." Whether one thoroughly appreciated West's timing or not (or even believed that George Bush ever really cared about black people in the first place) he set off dialogues and prompted polls dealing with race (and poverty) much in the way the O. J. Simpson debacle did when it played itself out nationally. West also did not spare the media from criticism, pointing out its biased reporting of the chaos in New Orleans (for example, captioned pictures describing blacks as "looting" and whites as "finding" food stuff). America once again had to confront its own unalloyed racialist baggage even during a national crisis.

My own appreciation for hip hop music and culture stems from its unabashed articulation of the most distressing issues facing my generation and a younger generation—often referred to as the millennium generation—that has grown up in hip hop's wake. The list of social ills and sexual contradictions confronting the hip hop and millennium generations boggles the mind. Varyingly defined as those born between 1965 and 1984 or more broadly, as the post–civil rights, post-segregation generation,[2] the hip hop generation in particular is attempting to explore and affirm its sexuality in an era rife with pornography, the mainstreaming of strip clubs, and the sexualization of everything from blue jeans ads to prime-time television. They are also simultaneously running up against chronic unemployment, mind-numbing poverty, affirmative action backlash, police brutality, the growth of the prison-industrial complex, the HIV/AIDS pandemic, the continued war on drugs, and increasing suicide rates, violence, and despair. It is no wonder that irreverence, that old standby of youth, and "girls (and boys) gone (sexually) wild" appear to be the hallmarks of hip hop.

* * *

As a cultural phenomenon, rap music made its appearance in the late 1970s with artists like Melle Mel and Lady B. The music could be first heard at youth centers, DJ battles, and house parties in the predominantly black and brown communities of the South and West Bronx. By the 1980s, hip hop music swept across the nation and captured the socio-political realities of youth from New York to Los Angeles to Chicago to New Orleans. By the 1990s, the music was ubiquitous. The gangsta funk of Dr. Dre's solo album *The Chronic* altered the commercial landscape of gangsta rap music. And in 1998 the unprecedented five Grammy wins of rapper Lauryn Hill for *The Miseducation of Lauryn Hill* flew in the face of critics who had long ago dismissed the music as a fad. Indeed, upon ascending to the podium to claim her Grammy for Album of the Year, an incredulous Hill responded, "This is crazy . . . this is hip hop."

Due to technological innovations, consumer capitalism, and media and entertainment mergers, hip hop naturally expanded beyond its DJing, MCing, break dancing, and tagging origins. The hip hop universe soon included fashion, fiction, movies, and magazines. Frat parties on predominantly white campuses like Vanderbilt and Stanford universities suddenly had hip hop twists, from "CEOs and Corporate Ho's," to "Pimps and Ho's," to "G.I. Joe and Barbie Ho." Homecoming performance invitations were extended to rap acts like Busta Rhymes, Chingy, and the Ying Yang Twins.

Even politics has not been immune to hip hop's tentacle-like grasp. Dissent and critique have long been a cornerstone of hip hop, though it is clear that the collective political agenda of this generation is still a nascent one. Materialistic and hypercommodified, any political ideals put forth by this generation risk co-optation as fashionable. As hip hop culture comes to be increasingly marketed globally and identified as mainstream, its more progressive political ambitions, like those signified by the 2004 and 2006 National Hip Hop conventions, will continue to face serious challenges.[3]

Indeed, Marc Anthony Neal captures the political "ironies" faced by progressive hip hop generation artists such as Talib Kweli, the Black-Eyed Peas, Sista Souljah, and Common: "[T]his generation . . . speaks to the ironies of hip hop itself—an art form that seeks to neither delegitimize nor undermine the logics of late-stage capitalism, but rather to reorient those logics to serve the interests of its constituents. It's not a perfect science."[4] No, it isn't. For as the late black feminist poet Audre Lorde cautioned about using the "master's tools to dismantle the master's house," consumer capitalism is in large part responsible for the huge race and class disparities about which hip hop artists—progressive and not —wax poetic.

According to the Recording Industry Association of America and the market research firm NPD Group, hip hop CD sales amounted to $1.7 billion in 2002 and $1 billion in 2003, while hip hop's popularity as a musical genre garnered 13.8 percent of the market.[5] Despite its dominance in CD sales and cultural influence, for some—like cultural critic Stanley Crouch and jazz great Wynton Marsalis—hip hop music and culture continues to inhabit the profane and ridiculous. Hip hop is especially lacking, they say, when compared to that other genre of race-transcending music honed by black musicians and singers—jazz.

In his essay collection, *The Artificial White Man: Essays on Authenticity,* Crouch, an acclaimed essayist and consummate jazz and blues devotee, "spanks" hip hop artists and

producers who dabble in what he deems hedonistic buffoon-
ery characteristic of D. W. Griffith's portrayals of blacks in
The Birth of a Nation. Crouch varyingly casts these offenders of taste and morals as "neo-Sambos" with their "mug-
ging or scowling" and "gold teeth, drop-down pants, and
tasteless jewelry." And from his roost at New York's *Daily
News*, Crouch has lobbed many a rock, brick, and bat at hip
hop (the titles of his articles include "Hip Hop's Thugs Hit
New Low," "Hip Hop Gets the Bruising It Deserves," "Hip
Hop Takes A Hit"). His latest verbal beat-down of hip hop,
in a January 23, 2005 piece in the *Daily*, manages to saddle
up to black women in their ensuing battle over images and
lyrics in hip hop. As a follow-up to his excoriating column
on the 2004 protest against Nelly's "Tip Drill" video at Spelman College, the not-always-chummy Crouch, particularly
in his editorializing on black women and American sexual
politics, writes in praise of *Essence* magazine:

> The magazine is the first powerful presence in the black me-
> dia with the courage to examine the cultural pollution that is
> too often excused because of the wealth it brings to knuckle-
> heads and amoral executives.
>   This anything-goes-if-sells attitude comes at a cost. The el-
> evation of pimps and pimp attitudes creates a sadomasochis-
> tic relationship with female fans. They support a popular id-
> iom that consistently showers them with contempt.

Crouch touches upon the very ethos that has gradually consumed the most popular expressions of hip hop's gender politics: a most debasing duet of female adulation and sacrifice
in the face of misogyny and misanthropy.

    Just as rabble rousing and critical, his Lincoln Center

colleague Wynton Marsalis regards hip hop performers as "entertainers" not "artists." In a 2003 interview with *The Guardian* ("Blowing Up a Storm"), he suggests that hip hop is a "new minstrel show," a caricature, with "rappers, calling each other niggas and bitches." For Marsalis such images peddle racism and "the youth are fooled, and a lot of money is being made." Crouch and Marsalis believe hip hop is all loutish dissonance, a cacophonous mess, while jazz embodies at once a black aesthetic and the enduring principles of American democracy that emphasize a harmonious union of seemingly cacophonous sounds and people.

In the United States and abroad, jazz, with its origins in blues, has inspired and continues to inspire generations of artists, writers, and activists. In the wake of the music, a unique style, attitude, fashion, and language followed. Jazz also had a sexual dimension. It was imagined to be emanating from the free and funky way that only black folks made love. It also had its political dimension, and indeed, Billie Holiday's "Strange Fruit," "God Bless the Child," and "Good Morning, Heartache," to name a (very) few, tell tales of depression, poverty, and state-sanctioned lynching.

The innovation of jazz artists moved jazz from the margins to the center of American life as a unique and authentic American musical genre. Although jazz record sales represent only roughly 2 percent of the total market, jazz has become sacred. Centers for jazz studies nestled on elite university campuses have cropped up. In 2003, the International Association of Jazz Educators' conference in Toronto drew ten thousand participants. There is also Jazz at Lincoln Center as well as commercial and academic books, not to mention the PBS-funded Ken Burns documentary on jazz. (Resistance to jazz's legitimacy, of course, still rears its head. The brouhaha over jazz violinist Regina Carter playing Niccolo Paganini's Cannon in Genoa, Italy, was as much about jazz's race and class origins as Italian nationalism—the fear of the "Coca-Cola-lization" of Italy by American culture.)

And so while jazz has become sacred, hip hop still dawdles, for some, in the profane. This is despite Harvard University's having housed the Hip Hop Archives (now at Stanford with Professor Marcyliena Morgan), hip hop's arrival at the Smithsonian, and Pulitzer and Nobel prize-winning novelist Toni Morrison's hip hop rendition of Aesop's *Fables* in her children's books. Hip hop, like jazz, has also made serious inroads in France with the emergence of French rap and *rai* music in Paris and Marseille. And here we return to the intent of this book. Notwithstanding its incipient political agenda, scholarly legitimacy, and progressive cadre of artists and thinkers, the profane in hip hop culture has come to be identified as its public face and voice. This profanity is tied to its raunchy street lyrics, nihilism, prepackaged "thuglite" recipes for commercial success, and gender foibles.

* * *

Hence, *Pimps Up, Ho's Down* continues to take our national banter on hip hop culture in a gender-inclusive direction. This is a book about young women and hip hop culture. More specifically, the book addresses the male-dominated culture of hip hop and the various ways in which young black women connect with that culture. It is about a new gender politics that hip hop has helped to define. While many believe we know exactly who's down with hip hop in its present "pimps up" transmutation—the groupies, the strippers, the video vixens—here I tease that out. In fact, I believe it's a provocative cultural commentary that makes a case for hip hop's commercial success as heavily dependent upon young black women. Overexposed young black female flesh, "pimpin'," "playin'," "sexin'," and "checkin'" in videos, television, film, rap lyrics, fashion, and on the Internet, is indispensable to the mass-media-engineered appeal of hip hop culture, which is helping to shape a new black gender politics.

This is not a book that chronicles rap lyrics and sexism. That line of inquiry has been vigorously pursued and will continue to be a touchstone for dialogue about hip hop generation men and misogyny, as it has been with *Essence* magazine's "Take Back the Music" campaign and before that the late civil rights activist Dr. C. Delores Tucker's much poohpoohed anti-rap crusades. It is not a "who's who" of hip hop women artists or a history of hip hop in general, although it will touch upon all of these matters. (For a discussion of women's trailblazing roles in hip hop, I refer the reader to *Vibe's Hip-Hop Divas* and black feminist writer Gwendolyn Pough's standard-bearing *Check It, While I Wreck It,* 2004).

Rather *Pimps Up, Ho's Down* aims to cast the net wider and deeper on hip hop culture and young black women. As a feminist writer of the hip hop generation, I cannot help but question the complexities of young black women's engagement with hip hop culture. I recognize that the madness visited upon hip hop generation black women comes as much from within their own communities as from without.

Sexual violence, sexism, "beat-downs," sexual dishonesty, anti-lesbianism, and the legacy of color prejudice all hammer away at self-esteem.[6] Most young black women experience at least one of these challenges. This book attempts to explicate where hip hop culture contributes to these distinctly female difficulties. It is not that these issues never existed before the hip hop global takeover. But the very public celebration and commercial trafficking in such images and behaviors has made them appear normal, acceptable, and entertaining. That young black men face their own set of challenges is undeniable; patriarchal and misogynistic notions of manhood and masculinity combined with racism have deeply impacted the ways in which men interact both with one another and with women. These interactions have currency in hip hop and thus greatly inform this book.

Critical questions guiding my work include the following: How has color prejudice permeated hip hop culture? How has mainstream beauty culture, primarily through hip hop music videos, impacted young black women? How have hip hop's lyrics and visual riffs on the acrimonious and sexually charged nature of male-female relationships encouraged the sexual abuse of young black women?

Pimps Up, Ho's Down also tackles head-on two other issues. The first is hip hop's increasing alliance with the $10 billion a year adult entertainment industry through the glorification of strip clubs in hip hop–oriented movies, videos, and music. Artists like Snoop Dogg, Ice-T, Mystikal, and N.E.R.D. have even released pornographic videos, and in some cases compact discs are accompanied by X-rated DVDs and songs not featured on the album. Hip hop's association with the sexually explicit has led to the 2002 and 2005 VH1 sponsored documentaries: "Hip-Hop and Hot Sex" and "Hip-Hop Videos and Sexploitation on the Set," respectively. The implications for young black women and girls are less than optimal. When Snoop Dogg gave up hosting the Euro-focused *Girls Gone Wild* videos to launch a 1-900 number and *Snoop's Doggystyle*—winner of an Adult Entertainment Award—he explained his reason in that "keep it real" logic that has come to define this new black gender politics: "No black girls, no Spanish girls—all white girls. And that ain't cool, because white girls ain't the only hos that get wild."[7]

Second is the rise of groupie culture in the hip hop world. This culture is not restricted to women. Tales are legion of black male groupies and the homoerotic and homophobic tensions their presence incites. But for our purposes, black women and groupie culture will remain the focus of *Pimps Up, Ho's Down*. Of the many roles young black women play in hip hop, one of the most rapped about is the groupie. Groupies have always had their part to play in the entertainment industry. But prior to hip hop, young black women were considered bit players in the groupie scene despite their prevalence among the jazz, blues, funk, and soul set. Mass media and the mainstreaming of hip hop culture have teamed up, however, to expose young black women's willing participation in sex escapades. Lying prostrate or on bended knees, black groupies are an essential cog in the "playa-pimp-ho-bitch" gearshift of hip hop culture. Like wet wipes, they are convenient and disposable. Indeed, our generation has witnessed the steady emergence of a hip hop groupie culture as a crucial part of the larger hip hop culture. Unfortunately, many of these young black women see their versions of "girls gone wild" as the fruit of women's sexual liberation.

At this juncture I would be remiss to not take on the rabidly heterosexist nature of hip hop. In this near compulsory heterosexual culture, women are routinely reduced to conquests and objects. What are the possibilities and challenges for young, black lesbians, those "not so strictly dickly" women? Because hip hop culture is generally filtered through a lens of heterosexuality and posturing around masculinity, same-sex-loving women have been generally co-opted into the male fantasy of a ménage à trois on the order of Ludacris's "Splash Waterfalls" video from his album *Chicken-N-Beer.* In "Splash Waterfalls," female sexual arousal and coupling is arbitrated electronically by a virile male presence (for example, Ludacris on computer screen).

Interestingly, a study conducted by Motivational Educational Entertainment, *This Is My Reality: The Price of Sex: An Inside Look at Black Urban Youth Sexuality,* which summarized findings from forty focus groups across nine cities in 2002, found that there is increased openness about young females having sex with other females. According to the study,

> Overwhelmingly, across all nine cities, [black urban] youth of both genders spoke openly about the increased occurrence of female-on-female sexual relationships (i.e., lesbianism) in their schools, communities, and even in their own personal lives. . . . Overall, youth seemed to struggle with whether this phenomenon should be described as a "trend" or as something that is here to stay.[8]

Viewed through the prism of the hypermasculine culture of hip hop, lesbians and lesbianism are in some respects the final frontier of conquest. The prevailing mentality is that all lesbians need is a "good stiff one" to set them on a "straight" (or at the very least, bisexual) course. This idea was parodied, to a *fault,* some would say, by Spike Lee in *She Hate Me* with the help of "lesbian consultant" and *Village Voice* columnist Tristan Taormino. Taormino stopped Lee from throwing the film over the lesbian-fantasy precipice as he imagined a final scene with all three characters moving toward the bedroom. Though Lee aimed to force the audience to contemplate new configurations of the family (two fathers, one mother, two mothers, one father), that the film's major lesbian protagonists were of the "lipstick" variety and that *She Hate Me*'s final scene seemed to reproduce the ménage à trois fantasy with a kiss as opposed to intercourse, raised more than a few brows.

Failing co-optation, the words "lesbian," "butch," and "dyke" are usually hurled as epithets at women who do not respond to male sexual charisma, as in Lloyd Banks's "Groupie Love": "If shorty ain't feelin me shorty must like girls. . . . If the bitch don't like me the bitch must don't like men." Here women are cast as either groupies or lesbians. And while some female rappers who have achieved mainstream success, such as Lil' Kim, make clear that "I ain't gay, this ain't no lesbo flow" ("Get Money"). Others like Trina—Kim's Southern "get money" counterpart—tease that she's "quick to deep-throat the dick / And let another straight lick the clit" ("Nann-Nigga"), lyrics suggestive of a bisexual ménage à trois or a heterosexual threesome with Trina on both receiving ends. In this way the lesbian figure is used as a trans-gendered trope in hip hop culture. As the archetypal straw women, she is simultaneously a foil to male sexual endeavors (as rapper Trick Daddy asserted, "It just don't seem right for a woman not to want dick"[9]), a measurement of what is deemed culturally unfeminine, a testament, if "set straight," of the limitlessness of charismatic masculinity, and she is also a cock-tease for sybaritic heterosexual sex.

Flesh-and-blood black lesbians live, as do we all, much more complicated and fuller lives than depicted in rhyming couplets. And despite hip hop's heterosexism and homophobia, black lesbians have carved a space for themselves within the culture. Hip hop's various enterprises and intersections have long included athletes from Cheryl Swoopes to Cynthia Cooper, artists such as DJ Pam of the Coup, Miss Money, and Medusa, and filmmakers Yvonne Welbon, Doria Roberts, Aishah Simmons, Sidra Smith, and Tiona McClodden, festivals like Queerstock and the now-defunct woman- and gay-positive Black Lily Tour.

Many artists though, who are "closeted" or have one foot in and one foot out, have had to tolerate, oftentimes silently, slights and aspersions regarding their personhood and femininity. And so they must grit their teeth as they film, rap, sing, and write about every aspect of their triumphs and disappointments except those relating to their sexual being. All the while heterosexual artists gloat or wail about theirs. This arrangement demonstrates hip hop's glaring double standard regarding lesbians.

In the current national homophobic climate—tweaked by the gay/lesbian marriage debate and our "don't ask, don't tell" military policy—silence and secrecy in the industry prevails. Tiona McClodden, an Atlanta filmmaker and hip hop videographer who has worked with artists like Murder Inc. and Twista, relates that the situation for lesbians is especially precarious in the South:

> Some people only come out during pride and go back in. These are fragile times because of the political climate and religion in the South. You have to balance your art, private life and career. Since so much of southern hip hop is call and response, it can be really tough. Your sexuality can become the focus of a battle. Some women will adapt an extreme masculinity to get along, dress aggressively—then people respond to your lyrics. The problem is you are left with the very same sexism and misogyny of male rappers.[10]

In describing the climate for lesbian artists in the South, McClodden reveals the bind they face should they choose to "out" themselves. Their sexuality and private lives could potentially overshadow their artistic contributions. Should they conform to the ideals of black masculinity performed by their male peers in order to be taken seriously as artists, they risk duplicating the very male privilege that their presence on the hip hop scene is meant to disrupt. Underground hip hop artist Medusa, who lends her voice and song, "One Bad Sista," to Tina Andrews's animated film *Sistas 'N the City,* weighed in on the question of sexuality and artistry in *Curve* magazine: "I think people avoid speaking on that [lesbianism] because they don't want that to be the primary focus of who they are. Because that can dilute everything else."[11] It is not only with commercial hip hop that lesbiphobia is present, but even in the supposedly safe, progressive spaces of the underground. Tiona McClodden continues, "As opposed to being called 'dyke,' in mixed gendered underground spaces, the men talk to you like a pimp." McClodden reveals that male practices of heterosexism extend to include verbal versus overtly sexual conversions. Lesbians can be "talked straight" by a "conscious brother," and the moniker "queen" replaces "dyke."

Indeed, the merest intimation of female sexual desire outside the heterosexual paradigm sparks urban tales and bizarre panics such as singer Tweet and Missy Elliot's collabo, "Oops, Oh My!" with the verse: "I tried and I tried to avoid / but this thing was happening / Swallow my pride . . . But this body felt just like mine." In any case, that there are black lesbian hip hop artists is an open secret in the industry and the hip hop nation. Of course, the lesbiphobic lyrics that spew forth from the mouths of various underground and mainstream colleagues are troubling. Yet truth be told the most concentrated lesbiphobia and backlash—the kind that inspires compulsory silence—can be found among the multiracial, hip hop CD-purchasing public.

Like the "Golden Age" of Hollywood under the studio system where actors and actresses were often contractually discouraged from revealing their sexual orientation (Greta Garbo, Marlene Dietrich) or their marriages in order to maintain the illusion of their availability as partners or lovers (hence their box office draw) to the film-going public, many aspiring and mainstream hip hop artists play it straight for the public. In a patriarchal culture, women in the rap game too are molded like Pygmalion's Galatea, or better still, George Bernard Shaw's Eliza Doolittle and Spike

Lee's closeted lesbian rapper Evelyn (from the film *She Hate Me*) into the perfect strumpets of heterosexual hip hop generation male desire—"strictly dickly."

As much as the sexploitation of young black women is necessary to the "keep it real" mantra of hip hop artists, corporate bottom lines, and marketing strategies, we must acknowledge our own role in this troubling relationship. We are enthralled by hip hop culture, and we conspicuously (and happily) consume its primary products—music, fashion, and values. As Joan Morgan poignantly asserts, "women love hip hop—as sexist as it is—is 'cuz all that in-yo-face testosterone makes our nipples hard."[12] Young black women do in fact represent a core audience of hip hop consumers, as studies by the Center for AIDS Research at Emory University and Motivational Educational Entertainment reveal. The truism of the mass media, as demonstrated by everyone from conservative John McWhorter[13] to the decidedly left-of-center *Essence* magazine "Take Back the Music" campaign, is that white males are hip hop's core consumers. While Soundscan data may support these earnest claims, what such narrow coverage of hip hop's core audiences has effectively done is ignite national hand-wringing and hysteria among whites. This angst is linked to the perceived negative influence that hip hop has on America's youth (read: whites). The relationship of young black women to hip hop culture is just as fraught with complexities, but has only just begun to register on the national radar.

Though much of America remains oblivious, there are many that have tried to move the dialogue on hip hop culture and gender forward. These include widely read progressive feminist critics and activists like bell hooks, Johnetta Cole, Kierna Mayo, Rosa Clemente, Martha Diaz, Lisa Fager, Maya Rockeymore, Kimberlé Crenshaw, Tricia Rose, Beverly Guy-Sheftall, Raquel Rivera, Joan Morgan, Scheherazade and Salamishah Tillet, and filmmaker Aishah Simmons. *Essence* magazine's "Take Back the Music" campaign, spearheaded by Michaela Angela Davis, Cynthia Gordy, and Akiba Solomon, is but one example of engaged work from within the belly of the beast. We have seen town hall meetings around the country, including at Spelman College for women, and "Rap Sessions" on gender. Political organizations, such as the National Coalition of 100 Black Women and the Congressional Black Caucus, have gotten involved, and yes, even activists like Dr. C. Delores Tucker have all tried, regardless of how poorly their efforts have been received. But in this melee, we must not forget the voices of young black women themselves. Though as a country we often don't listen to them, rest assured, these women have plenty to say on matters that vitally concern them. A group of young women at Sarah Lawrence College attempted to launch a national protest from Howard University to Stanford University against rap music's misogyny. Spelman College undergraduates, led by Moya Bailey, met the scourge of the black media when they protested rapper Nelly's visit to their campus after the airing of "Tip Drill." But more often then not, these objections, like those of so many other young black women, are muffled by the music.

I hope to help turn down the volume, but amplify our understanding, with voices of young black women themselves. In the final chapter of the book, as I close with a discussion of feminism and hip hop culture, I offer insights from young black women on the various issues raised throughout the book. *Pimps Up, Ho's Down* attempts then to provide a space for young black women's voices to be heard in all of their complex contradictions, dissent, and complicity.

1

"I SEE THE SAME HO"

Video Vixens, Beauty Culture, and Diasporic Sex Tourism

Every other video . . .
I see the same ho
> —TUPAC (featuring Nate Dogg, YGD Tha
> Top Dawg), "All About U"

Watching the videos, you see the long curly hair
[and] think, "Man that would be nice to have
some long, curly hair."
> —SELA, eighteen-year-old undergraduate

Brazilian women are usually desirable, as often
women of mixed ethnicities are. . . . Our leaders
should make a law demanding intercultural
breeding to fill our planet . . . thus ending all the
world's problems.
> —ASKMEN.COM, Top 99 Most Desirable
> Women 2005

hen Michelle "Micki"
Burks decided to take on the role of eye candy in the now-
defunct rap-reggae group Ruff Neck Sound System's music
videos "Stick by Me" and "Luv Bump," little did she know
that her decision would land her years later in the category
of "video ho." Her performances in the music videos did
not involve provocative backside acrobatics, but her video

persona in "Luv Bump" is interestingly transmogrified into a "hoochie" by the video's end due to fast-living and hustling men. Shot in New York, the video aired in 1995 on the Rachel-hosted Black Entertainment Television format *Caribbean Rhythms.* At 5'8" with long brown highlighted hair and honey-toned skin, Micki attended the prestigious Berklee School of Music in Boston from 1986 to 1990. A soprano with a superb vocal range, she toured Europe and Japan, releasing an album called *Inca,* and then took up modeling with Models, Inc. in Boston as a side gig until her music career took off. She met the Ruff Neck crew in the Boston music scene. Her then-boyfriend, Chris, was a well-known producer who had teamed with such venerable acts as the late Donnie Hathaway's daughter Lahla.

When asked about the moniker "video ho," she emphatically rejects any description of her experiences as degrading. She does nonetheless lament the portrayals of women in hip hop videos of late, stating that, "It is unnecessary. They don't have to treat the women like that." When asked if she would work in the emerging lucrative music video industry today if the opportunity presented itself again, the still-lithe thirty-six-year-old says with a laugh, "Yeah, if I were thinner [and] as a model not a 'video ho.' "

While sales in the music industry continue a downward spiral that even the gestalt of rapper 50 Cent's *The Massacre* (which moved over one million units in just under four days) cannot break, the music video DVD has emerged as a boon to the recording industry. In an April 7, 2004, press release, Jay Berman, Chairman of IFPI (International Federation of the Phonographic Industry), an affiliate of the Recording

Industry Association of America (RIAA), the organization responsible for the world's largest music market, noted that music video sales are rapidly becoming an important revenue stream for the industry. The music video, popularized by the launch of cable television stations such as Black Entertainment Television (BET), Music Television (MTV), and Video Hits 1 (VH1), represents the lion's share of formatting for these stations. Launched in 1980, 1981, and 1985 respectively, the first popular music video to debut on MTV was The Buggles's "Video Killed the Radio Star," a video that predicted rather prematurely that the music video genre would supplant the radio. Music videos have exploded, with budgets as large as some indie film projects, more developed narratives and sets, and digital technology, which has also allowed for a clearer picture and a larger than life celluloid image.[1] The hip hop music video in particular also provides brand product placement with a bumping beat. Like a four- to six-minute advertisement, the music video DVD sells music and the fabulous lifestyle signified by whatever material acquisitions are worn (or not), driven, or drank within its frames—all at a general sticker price between thirteen and eighteen dollars. Borrowing from cultural critic Greg Tate's observations on hip hop culture in "Nigs R Us, or How Blackfolk Became Fetish Objects," the hip hop video has "collapsed art, commerce, and interactive technology into one mutant animal."[2] Similar to the film industry, which ties its potential box office take to A-list stars as well as well-known directors, the directors of music videos have become a highly sought after group, particularly veterans such as Hype Williams, Paul Hunter, Little X, and Chris Robinson.[3]

Recording artists recognize that the music video can make or break a career, and heavy rotation on MTV, BET, and VH1 all but guarantees break-out success. Indeed, 70 percent of BET's programming, the go-to station for urban hip hop generationers, is music videos and infomercials. And the cable station reaches some eighty million homes.[4]

In "All about U," a Tupac Shakur, Nate Dogg, and YDG Tha Top Dawg collaboration, the rap artists bond over their disdain for "video ho's" and "groupies" who they encounter in every city they tour and video they see. Like Micki, many of these women are singers, professional models, dancers, and aspiring actresses, earning their rent, tuition monies, or commercial exposure for a day's work on a shoot. And some dance and shake for free for their five minutes of fame, jumping in front of the camera when Young Buck or any one of the St. Lunatics roll up on a North Nashville or North St. Louis block with a film crew in tow. As Atlanta hip hop industry insider and videographer Tiona McClodden suggests, "Many of the background video models use their bodies as demos because they know that much of what is shot will be left on the floor of the editing room. They have one opportunity. If they do something provocative enough to stand out, they anticipate that the shot just may remain in the final video."[5] That the impact of these sexually suggestive videos is undeniably regressive in terms of gender politics and young girls and women's self-identity is revealed in a 2003 year-long study conducted by the Center for AIDS Research (CFAR) at Emory University. Tracking 522 Alabama girls' hip hop video consumption and behaviors, the study revealed that a higher consumption of hip hop videos corresponded negatively with higher frequency of sexually transmitted diseases, alcohol and drug abuse (60 percent), and multiple sex partners (twice as likely).

* * *

But just as important as the complex motivations behind young women's suggestive performances in hop-hop videos —rumps moving with the alacrity of a jackhammer, hips gyrating like a belly dancer on amphetamines, limbs akimbo, mouths agape in a perpetual state of the orgasmic "oh"—is the repetition of particular ideals of femininity. Hip hop is now as much about images as it is skills and beats. That the vast majority of the young women in these videos are either fairer-skinned, ethnically mixed, or of indeterminate ethnic/racial origins, with long, straight, or curly hair would suggest that along with the stereotype of hypersexuality and sexual accessibility, a particular type of beauty is offered up as ideal. In some respects, the majority of these women represent what historian Tiffany Patterson calls "ascriptive mulattas," that is, those whose physical beauty transcends characteristics such as darker hues, full lips, and the like, historically prefigured as less than ideal (non-European). The "mulatta" figure, a pejorative term if ever there was one, is typically depicted as tragic because of her "in-between" racial status. Yet the "mulatta" has also been deemed in literary and film annals as the most ideal in the arena of feminine beauty, and the secretly longed for in the heterosexual marketplace of desire. This status comes about precisely because of her mixed-race heritage involving some configuration of "black" and "white," which in the European and

American male imagination signals the perfect blending of skillfulness in matters of sex (read: black) and physical beauty (read: white).

The physical appeal to both white and black men of Gabrielle Union, Ciara, Beyoncé, and Tyra Banks falls into ascriptive mulatta territory, as did that of Lena Horne and Dorothy Dandridge—just ask the men at askmen.com where Union, Ciara, Banks, and Beyoncé are ranked among the 2006 edition of the top ninety-nine most desirable women. On any given segment of MTV's *Top Twenty,* or BET's *Rap City* and *106 & Park,* roughly 70 percent of the videos feature superbly toned, nubile, hybrid flesh. One could certainly argue that practically all seemingly black flesh in the "New World" is a hybrid given the history of transracial contact. But it is precisely because of the enormous *range* of blackness (as a result of consensual and non-consensual) sex that the incredibly narrow prototype of beauty is even more troubling.

As writer Kevin Powell argues in *Who's Gonna Take the Weight,* hip hop generationers still do not fully appreciate the range of black women's beauty. Even the fallout in the hip hop community from the 2002 Grammy Awards ceremony over Alicia Key's multiple Grammy wins over India Arie hinged unfortunately (and mistakenly I would add) for some on the issue of color. Another example is the ruckus over the fall 2004 season of *America's Next Top Model* (*ANTM*), a reality show that attempts to demystify high-fashion modeling by demonstrating that models, while born with certain assets like height, are primarily talent-development projects and that "can-do" attitudes go the distance. The show is undeniably in the service of beauty culture, which in general has been less accepting, if not hostile, to black women. However, in the 2004 season *ANTM* was UPN's highest-rated program among women ages eighteen to forty-nine as well as teens. As the network's newest cash cow, it was also one of the top ten programs among African American adults, and the highest-rated reality show among African Americans. Its host, übermodel Tyra Banks, consistently emphasizes personality over a particular "look." Nonetheless, the conclusion of the fall 2004 season caused viewer squabbles regarding the hair and skin color of the final two contestants, Yaya DaCosta Johnson and Eva Pigford. In an interview with *TV Guide*'s Daniel Coleridge, the runner-up, Yaya, a Brown University graduate, responded to the interviewer's perception of her "look" as "Afrocentric," a perception that may have contributed to her loss:

> I'm not Afrocentric, I'm just natural. But in this country, black women who don't straighten their hair with chemical processing are stereotyped and labeled. Not *all* black women with straight hair need chemical processing, but I would have to to achieve that look. Just because we don't straighten our hair doesn't mean we're trying to be anything else—we're being ourselves. If anything hurts me about that, it's that I wasn't allowed the luxury of being myself like the other girls were. Nobody asks Cassie, Ann or Amanda to be "less white." I'm used to having to defend my very being. That makes me a little sensitive.[6]

DaCosta Johnson's browner skin and unprocessed hair moved her into an Afrocentric space when compared to Eva Pigford's African American girl-next-door look with chemically straightened hair, light eyes, and lighter hue.

DaCosta Johnson's predicament on *Top Model* raises old

questions in this new era on assimilation, identity, and beauty. And yet, the mixing bowl with a wee bit of nutmeg and cinnamon standard of beauty endorsed ostensibly by American culture (more specifically on Madison Avenue) parallels the shifting ideas of beauty in hip hop videos that are, some would argue, necessarily still derivative of a white ideal.

In "Generation E.A.: Ethnically Ambiguous," a feature in the Fashion & Style section of *The New York Times,* advertising executives and fashion magazine editors offered running commentaries that ranged from disquieting to just plain dim on marketing trends to "tweens," teens, and hip hop generationers in both the mainstream and high-end marketplace: "Today what's ethnically neutral, diverse, or ambiguous has tremendous appeal"; "What is perceived as good, desirable, successful is often a face whose heritage is hard to pin down"; "We're seeing more of a desire for the exotic, left-of-center beauty . . . [It] represents the new reality of America, which includes considerable mixing . . . It's the changing face of American beauty."[7] That racial categories are social constructs rather than biological realities—though this does not alter the lived experiences of those who occupy those categories—that "considerable" "race" mixing is not "a new reality" but has been historically widespread in the United States, and that America is not as "white" as it believes itself to be has been duly noted since at least the nineteenth century by writers and activists such as Frances Ellen Harper Watkins in her novel *Iola Leroy.* Even in *The Birth of a Nation,* a racist film posing as an American cinematic masterpiece, racial amalgamation is a core preoccupation because of its prevalence. The contemporary scholarly writing of philosophers of race Kwame Anthony Appiah and Naomi Zack are only a few examples of our awareness of the power of social constructs. Both Appiah and Zack have argued that "race" and therefore categories of race are biologically non-existent, dishonest, and in bad faith. That we as a culture cling to them relates more to our desires to enact and maintain social, political, and economic powers and privileges.

In effect, racial categories are themselves racist. In her 1993 book *Race and Mixed Race*, Zack argues presciently for the category of *gray*, an almost uncanny predecessor to "ethically ambiguous." Therefore, the excited tone of discovery evoked in the "Generation E.A." article seems more than a bit out of touch. The rhetoric that still situates whiteness at the center of American beauty culture and darker hues on this schematic shifting to the left (one wonders what right of center beauty looks like) quite simply reinforces a hierarchy of beauty, as well as the notion of fixed racial categories. Indeed, ethnic ambiguity does not guarantee racial ambiguity, particularly in relationship to those possessing "African" ethnicities and origins. One may be ethnically mixed (ambiguous) but racially marked as black.

Despite the hubbub about Generation E.A., editors and ad executives admit that whiteness continues to dominate the beauty and fashion industries. Where does, pray tell, such a hierarchy leave Generation Non-E.A. (non–ethnically ambiguous) black women? In her widely read book *Beauty Myth*, Naomi Wolf relates how the beauty industry essentially creates angst in women regarding their choices—Yaya

DeCosta Johnson, for example. While not a treatise against the beauty industry and practices of adornment (though some critics have reductively read the book as Wolf's feminist cri de coeur against lipstick wearing), *The Beauty Myth* in fact argues for something very basic: a women's right to choose. Wolf makes the radical assertion that women should choose how they want to look, without fear of employment discrimination, or of being castigated as unfeminine, or of being subjected to the litany of other charges leveled at those whose beauty practices (or lack thereof) run counter to dominant ideas about what it means to be a woman.

Women who choose not to indulge in beauty practices are often disadvantaged and made to feel guilty for their lack of conformity in a culture that overemphasizes physical appearance. Simultaneously women who embrace beauty products and their images still "second guess" themselves and are subject to descriptions such as "high maintenance" and "not natural." And those women who embrace beauty culture and also fall outside the current rage over Generation E.A. or Ascriptive Mulattas are left to endlessly negotiate a maze of images and ideas that are not especially affirming and seem, at each turn, to lead to a dead end.

* * *

As with the behavioral implications for hip hop video consumption, the collision between hip hop culture and beauty culture, the marketing and packaging of the "same" video girl who resembles the high-fashion model who resembles the latest Hollywood "It" girl, also has a clear and deleterious impact on what young black female consumers come to identify as desirable. And the desire to be desirable seems especially costly and laborious for young black women, as the product-hawking, image-projecting hip hop video pumps cash into the mainstream and hip hop's multibillion-dollar fashion and beauty industries. In effect, what young black women cannot be, they now buy.

Who can forget the purchased artifices of Lil' Kim? Her "so unpretty" motivations for doffing and donning colored contact lens, purported skin-lightening procedures, nose contourings, platinum hair, breast augmentation, and liposuction. The visceral pain she articulated watching her Svengali-lover-father figure and public and very private abuser, the Notorious B.I.G., marry the lighter-skinned, fairer-maned hip hop/R&B singer Faith Evans nine days after meeting her.[8] Or the cracks of insecurity seeping from her admission: "Halle Berry, Sally Richardson, Stacy Dash, Jada Pinkett? I used to wish I looked like them motherfuckers!"?[9] On the question of breast augmentation, she says, "I laughed at first. But then I went home and really thought about it. I went to the best, most expensive doctor available, but that was the most pain I ever felt in my life."[10]

As with Lil' Kim, the overwhelming majority of us black and Latina women offer our labor in a marketplace—one that still does not pay us equally—in order to purchase some happiness through beauty.[11] (The median weekly earnings of black women who worked full time in 2001 was $451 compared with $521 for white women, $518 for black men, and $694 for white men; these figures are for non-college-educated black women; in 2004, college-educated black women, roughly two million, outearned both the white women and

Latinas.) Using data from over three thousand households surveyed by the Department of Commerce, marketers and corporations have determined that black women, with their increasing income, have the most influence on the growth in African American spending. Between 2001 and 2002, our spending on personal care products increased (by 18 percent), as did our expenditures on women's apparel and footwear (2 percent and 13 percent, respectively). Our generosity with ourselves was rivaled only by our generosity with others, as gift spending spiked by 155 percent.[12]

The July 2004 report released by *The U.S. Multicultural Women Market* suggests that the buying power of multicultural women (defined as African American, Asian American, and Hispanic American) will exceed $1 trillion by 2008 and African American women over eighteen years of age will keep the dominant share of the market. African American women's educational attainment is high; we are more confident and secure with ourselves, and one in four of us occupy professional or managerial positions. Yet, we are simultaneously least likely to be married (as our race loyalties tend to constrain our options) or even in fulfilling relationships with a female partner; dieting and exercise appear less of a concern while health risks are high. We are also very brand conscious, loyal, and receptive—or vulnerable, depending on your interpretation of the data—to media, and particularly to television.

Savvy marketers will continue to pitch products that seem to tap into our greatest strengths and deepest insecurities about beauty and desirability. Hair-care products accounted for $174 million of our disposable income in 2002.[13] Plastic surgery, once the strict domain of white women and a taboo subject, is now democratized and featured prominently in the same headline as the words "black or African American" in magazines and online portals such as *Essence, Newsweek,* and *AOL Black Voices* (though most African American women seek surgeries for breast reduction and tummy tucks). These spending trends on beauty and fashion have been chalked up to "African-American women hav[ing] finally just decided that it's time to love ourselves" by *Essence* beauty editor Miki Taylor.[14] While Asian American women also spend a great deal, more even, on fashion and beauty products and are just as brand conscious, they are also the leading consumers among women of financial services.[15] One wonders if our "loving ourselves" reflects our "security and confidence," or, given our marked receptivity to *all* media, our insecurity and self-doubt bred by the confluence of media, beauty, and hip hop culture? Shouldn't the slicing away, camouflage, and enhancement offered by plastic surgery and beauty products considered part of this new phenomenon of "loving ourselves" include a concomitant uptick in financial investments as well as diet- and exercise-related spending given our health risks? Purchased beauty is undeniably a depreciating asset, while health and financial solvency guarantees some degree of longevity. And yet, I am clearly aware that there are those hip hop generation women who would argue that if beauty enhancement lands you a "baller," it was money well spent.

In the end, despite all the hype about diversity and Generation E.A., hegemony prevails. Blondes, the stand-in for unadulterated whiteness, still have more fun. Generation E.A.

comes in at quite a distant second, and Generation A.M (Ascriptive Mulattas)—those left-of-center beauties—clinch third. Those of us who remain—the *un*aesthetically pleasing, racially marked plebeians, or Generation B (read: black)— anchor the bottom or the far left of the beauty schema, particularly with respect to mainstream culture.

Hip hop culture as represented through the "video vixens" and Madison Avenue collide on the beauty hierarchy in the ambiguous space between generations E.A. and A.M. And who determines the contours of this space? More often than not, it is black men. Besides sports—which has generated a cottage industry of books on the black male athlete—hip hop culture represents another cultural terrain dominated and shaped by black men. Certainly Erica Kennedy's hilarious debut novel *Bling!,* a tale of the hip hop industry, offers interesting commentary on black men as cultural brokers of desire who resemble modern-day Svengalis as they develop, control, and project what is desirable and equally cultivate the public's desire for E.A. and A.M. artists who nonetheless read "black."[16] In Kennedy's make-believe world that seamlessly channels the contradictions of hip hop culture, darker skin among women is a handicap to be overcome; dreaded, braided, or "happy to be nappy" hair are "no-no's"; and "big," as in body type, is definitely not beautiful.

Lest one get the impression that those women who self-identify as black and fall into the E.A. and A.M. categories of desirability do not also contend with demons not of their own making, they do. Idealization is often accompanied by alienation, "trophied" status, and petty jealousies. Anita Lewis, former Communications/Public Relations Liaison for

Pennsylvania State Senator Vincent Hughes and one of *Philadelphia Business Journal*'s "40 Under 40," admits that being a lighter-skinned black woman has its own challenges:

> The fighting began in middle school with other girls pulling my hair, trying to put glue in it, and taking swipes, with their fingernails, at my face. As a professional, there are those who think I have landed certain positions because of my looks. Undoubtedly, there are those who may perceive me as less threatening, more acceptable. I cut my hair extremely short at one point in my career so that people, especially men, would take me seriously, stop fixating on my hair and listen to what I was saying. My looks may have allowed my foot in the door, but my talents and skills keep me there.[17]

Singer Beyoncé Knowles, part of a roundtable discussion with other professional black women featured in *Newsweek,* also spoke to these very issues of color and beauty and her experiences as a lighter-skinned black woman. Knowles, who is incidentally identified as part of "Generation E.A." in *The New York Times* article, ranked number eight on 2005's askmen.com's top ninety-nine, and somersaulted Jennifer Lopez off the "booty pedestal" with her "Bootylicious" anthem and appearance on *Q* magazine's cover with the headline, "The Ass that Shook the World," offered: "Well, I could complain about being light-skinned. But that's life. People judge you by the way you look, unfortunately. . . ."[18]

So while black men may have questionable standards of beauty for black women, they are not, unlike Madison Avenue, necessarily worshipping at the altar of white beauty. They linger rather, as I have suggested, somewhere between Generation E.A. and Generation A.M. That heterosexual black youth culture leans toward "left-of-center beauty" is a direct result of the political landscape, ideology, and social gains offered by both the civil rights and black power movements. While integration offered by the civil rights movement presented access to corridors, classrooms, and bedrooms heretofore inaccessible, the 1970s' slogan "Black Is Beautiful" carried over into the 1980s and helped shape the worldview of the hip hop generation. It is not so much that black is no longer beautiful but too familiar. The forbidden-fruit aura once enveloping white women has also been thoroughly demystified as they too avail themselves of the most hedonistic offerings of hip hop culture, ergo the pornographic videos *Girls Gone Wild* with Snoop Dogg and *Groupie Love* with G-Unit. Moreover, beauty culture's stoking of white women's obsession with thinness, the aim for 103 lbs. whether one is 5'1" or 5'10", disinvites the development of "junk in the trunk," those protuberant charms essentialized in hip hop culture. Most white women are left "assed out."

Besides breeding misogyny and sexism, a surprising ancillary effect of such black male privilege and familiarity has been the desire for the unknown, the "exotic" feminine ideal. The ideal woman is indeed black-derived, curvy, and "thick," but she is "paprika'd" and salted with difference, as with the October 2004 Black-Irish-Cherokee-Asian "Eye Candy" centerfold in the hip hop magazine *XXL,* or December 2004's African-American-Egyptian-Brazilian "Eye Candy" spread. Beginning at opposite ends of the great chain of beauty's color spectrum, hip hop culture and mainstream beauty culture meet somewhere in the middle in their fetishization of ethnic brewing.

The desire for the unknown, the exotic and highly ethnically seasoned black woman of late has been satiated beyond U.S. borders—namely among the black diaspora in countries like Brazil. The mirror of Brazil is being reflected back on U.S. women. This latest "desire for the exotic," as the Generation E.A. article put it, then transcends not only "rigid social categories of race, class," but U.S. borders as well. Raquel Rivera has skillfully argued in *New York Ricans in the Hip-Hop Zone* that Latinas as the *buttapecans,* the *mamis,* have often served as the exotic detour in the predominantly black male world of hip hop. The interesting reality is that they too have now become part of "The Known World" (borrowing Edward P. Jones's Pulitzer prize-winning novel's title). The search for the beautiful is now in the *favelas* (the ghettos) of Brazil. Hence it is no small surprise to see advertisements by Game, Inc., a company based out of Las Vegas, Nevada, for the porn collection *Hip-Hop Honeys: Brazil Boom Boom,* "with the bootylicious bodies that make Brazil a fantasy favorite for the hip hop generation" in "hip hop on a higher level" magazines like *XXL* (see p. 41).[19]

In some respects, hip hop generation African American men's latest fetish parallels Brazil's own fetishizing of racial admixture as embodied by the mulatta figure. In a country where a cliché on the order of "white woman to wed, mulatta to bed, black woman to work" is befitting, Alma Guillermoprieto, author of *Samba,* notes:

> *Mulatas* are glorified sex fetishes, sanitized representations of what whites view as the savage African sex urge, but they are also, of course, tribute and proof of the white male's power: his sexual power, and his economic power, which allowed

him to wrest the *mulata*'s black mother away from her black partner. At the same time the *mulata* serves to perpetuate one of the myths that Brazilians hold most dear, that there is no racism in Brazil, that miscegenation has been natural and pleasant for both parties, that white people really, sincerely, do like black people. In fact, the aesthetic superiority accorded to light-skinned black women—*mulatas*—underlines the perceived ugliness of blacks before they have been "improved" with white blood. The white skin also serves to lighten a sexual force that in undiluted state is not only threatening but vaguely repulsive, and at the same time, the myth goes, irresistible.[20]

The fleshy hips, thighs, ample posterior, and thrust-forward breasts of the mulatta figure is offered as a sign of all things Brazilian, specifically Rio de Janeiro, as is Sugar Loaf, Corcovado (the Jesus Christ statue reigning majestically high above the city of Rio de Janeiro), the historic district of Lapa, Capoeira, and the *favelas*. As if taking cues from its northerly American neighborhoods, racial and ethnic brewing is celebrated but whiteness dominates the high-end billboards of Ipanema and the beauty industry. In interviewing a model talent scout for a May 2005 article on Brazil entitled "Beauty and the Beach," *Condé Nast Traveler* writer Julia Chapin uncovered that "right now what's hot are girls who have a European face but the body movements and attitude of a Latin." The talent scout admits that "dark-skinned girls from northern Brazil have a harder time getting work."[21]

The summer of 2003 brought the upbeat, radio-ready "Beautiful" collaboration between Snoop Dogg, Pharrell, and Uncle Charlie Wilson, formerly of the Gap Band. We all

Courtesy of Game Video, Inc. Hip-Hop Honeys name and logo and all contents of this advertisement are © Game Video, Inc.

sang along in Pharrell's Marvin Gaye–esque falsetto, ignoring the first refrain offered by Snoop about "Long hair, wit'cha big fat booty." By the time Snoop arrived at, "Black and beautiful, you the one I'm choosin' / Hair long and black and curly like you're Cuban," some black women were singing, "No, No, No, No!" instead of "Yeah, Yeah, Yeah, Yeah!"—mocking the Pharrell and Charlie Wilson refrain. The heavily rotated Chris Robinson–directed video was shot on location in Brazil. Stunning because of the locale and the women, "Beautiful" the video provides a visual representation of the new black feminine ideal in hip hop culture with the charge to "Look far Southward!" to find it. Surrounded by a bevy of Brazilian beauties, Snoop and Pharrell move through this postcard-like sonata, showcasing the history of New World race mixing of imported African captives, indigenous Indians, and conquering Europeans. While some have argued that the video vixens were not *Brasilieras,* the fact of the matter is that the video provides the illusion of an authentic Brazilian experience. The video has become perhaps the best advertisement the Brazilian travel and tourism industry could hope for in its recent attempts to tap into a specifically African American market.

Snoop is not the first hip hop artist to use Brazil and its women as backdrops, nor will he be the last. Indeed, southern rapper T.I. finds himself in Rio among frolicking women on Copacabana Beach in his 2006 "Why You Wanna" video. The Neptunes, the Pharrell Williams–Chad Hugo hit-making duo, acted in *Dude: We're Going to Rio,* the 2003 hip hop musical comedy directed by C. B. Harding. In this campy tale of love at first sight, Pharrell sees a travel poster for Brazil featuring a Brazilian woman with whom he falls in love, and he travels to Rio de Janeiro to find her. Ja Rule's video "Holla, Holla," directed by Hype Williams and from the 1999 CD *Venni Vetti Vicci,* broke ranks at the time of its release by featuring Brazilian women and shooting on location in Brazil. In an interview with AllHipHop.com, Ja Rule relates that

> At that point in Hip-Hop, it was still about your n*ggas in the videos with you. We flew out to Brazil, and it was magic instantly. We set up cameras, scouting ladies. There were mad beautiful chicks coming to the camera, and on the beach topless. All types of shit, man! I was extra amped! We turned the cameras on, and girls started flocking. We only brought one professional girl (Gloria Velez), and the rest were just girls from Brazil that wanted to get down.[22]

While "Holla, Holla" is an anthem to the rough-and-tumble life of thugdom, playin' bitches and poppin' snitches, "Beautiful" is purposely G-rated commercial fare, untarnished by bleeps; it is an ode to beauty by one of hip hop culture's legendary gangsta pimps, Snoop Dogg, a purveyor of style, a barometer for "what" and "who" is the "in" thing to do and screw.

When revolutionary writer Frantz Fanon wrote in his 1963 "handbook of the Black Revolution," *The Wretched of the Earth,* of "the pitfalls of national consciousness" and globalization with respect to developing nations and tourism, who would have imagined how prophetic his pronouncements were? And who would have thought that hip hop generation black men would join the Western bourgeois tourist "avid for the exotic . . . the beaches of Rio, the little

Brazilian . . . girls . . . , [t]he banking magnates, the techno-crats, and the big businessmen of the United States [who] have only to step onto a plane and they are wafted into sub-tropical climes, there for a space of a week or ten days to luxuriate in . . . delicious depravities"?[23] Despite harrowing statistics about poverty, unemployment, incarceration, HIV/AIDS, and drug use, hip hop generation black men have been able to access, generate, and benefit from the unprece-dented wealth that has made the United States the most powerful capitalist nation in the world.

The Selig Center for Economic Growth's survey *The Mul-ticultural Economy 2004* reports that African Americans have enjoyed a steady rise in income, resulting in $723 bil-lion in buying power as of September 2004, an increase of 3.9 percent over the $631 billion earned in 2002 as re-ported in the 2003 Target Market News' analysis *The Buy-ing Power of Black America*. This extraordinary wealth gen-eration has allowed them the means and opportunity to act in many respects with the same arrogance and license as their white American and European male contemporaries and the imperialist tourists of Fanon's era.

Latin America, Fanon wrote, is "Europe's brothel," and Brazil, in particular, has become to the heterosexual black American male what Tahiti was to the nineteenth-century painter Paul Gauguin—an idyllic place where one could "fuck, tan, and eat," or *"baiser, bronzer et bouffer,"* as the French Club Med experience was once described. Accord-ing to a BBC report on sex tourism and prostitution in Brazil, sex work in Brazil is on the upswing, as Brazilian women and girls look for a way out of dire poverty. Brazil has been pressed into the role of purveyor of sex tourism

as a result of the void left by Asia—specifically Thailand—
and the tsunami crisis. A casualty of its savvy and relentless
marketing, particularly with respect to women and sex, Brazil is identified as the land of samba, sensuality, the bikini
wax, and the Brazilian *bunda*, a string/thong bikini.[24] Such
are the obsessions with Brazilian sexuality that plastic sur-
geons offer a procedure called the Brazilian butt lift.[25] For a
few Brazilian *reais*, which amount to nominal amounts in
American dollars (and sometimes the promise of a better life
for Brazilians in the United States), one can experience the
fantasy that is Brazil—and generally from women from the
favelas.

In Brazil, the reputedly large parties thrown by moguls
such as Damon Dash and Sean "Puffy" Combs during Car-
nivale and the Brazilian fascination with all things Ameri-
cana, especially mass-produced and globally exported black
commodities such as music and music videos, provide cultural currency for hip hop generation black men that gives
them a Brazilian ghetto tour pass that includes discounts on
women. For those poor and working-class black men unable
to procure the fantasy on the ground, their imaginations,
like those writers of beguiling eighteenth- and nineteenth-
century travel narratives of exotic places and eager-to-be-
had women, will travel for them. For a mere $72 including
shipping and handling—a far cry from a $1,000 plane ticket
to Rio—they can be transported to Brazil via pornographic
visual aids like *Hip Hop Honeys: Brazil Boom Boom*'s
three-volume set and a poster.

In 2004, African Americans spent $4.6 billion on travel,
lodging, and transportation.[26] While the Caribbean and Africa have long been heavily marketed to African Americans

by the travel and tourism industry, partnerships between the Brazilian government and African American media moguls like *Essence* magazine founder Clarence Smith have resulted in deal-brokering between Varig Airlines and Avocet Travel and Entertainment that now includes direct flights from New York to Salvador, Bahia. Brazil represents an untapped market for African American businesses, and vice versa. As *Brazzil Online Magazine* suggests,

> This place (Brazil) has so much to offer African-Americans. Much more than any place on the continent of Africa. The environment here is stable; there is no civil war here. There are no famines on the scale of what a visitor would encounter in Africa. Brazil offers access to state of the art tele- communications, reliable banking systems, good roads and health facilities.[27]

Furthermore, the emergence of interest groups on the Web such as "African American Men & Brazilian Women" sig- nals the global inclinations and democratization of wander- lust and leisure afforded by the U.S. economic boom. Replete with visuals, The African American Men & Brazilian Women message board also provides insight into some of the kinds of leisure activities sought. There is a "do's and don'ts" list offered by one aficionado of Brazilian women. A sort of "Mr. Manners" for African American men traveling to Brazil, *ChgoBachelor31_4u* took his counsels from postings at Rio- exposed.com and Brazilmensclub.com, sites that promote sex tourism. Among other things, *ChgoBachelor31_4u* advises African American men not to "flirt with females unless your [*sic*] serious" or "go in the *favelas* unless your [*sic*] with someone you know & trust," but do "wear a condom," and "if your [*sic*] there (1) week you should average 10 females, if your [*sic*] there (2) weeks you should average 20 females," and finally, "Even if you dont [*sic*] need it fellas, 'blue devils' aka viagra. dont [*sic*] be ashamed to use it."[28]

For those interested in making "honest women" out the *Brasilieras, bgcaliber1* offers some handy tips as well:

1. Though it may be tough . . . try to see her a few times in Brazil b4 bringing her back. Learn some Portuguese (or bring someone who knows the language) and try to ask around her neighborhood what type of girl she is from the local guys (last thing you want to do is bring back a full fledged hoe). See how her family is (full of nice spiritual people or a group of thieves). Remember, the apple doesn't fall far from the tree.

2. If you do eventually get her here, do not trust her to visit other girlfriends living here by herself. KEEP HER AWAY FROM OTHER BRAZILIAN GIRLS HERE IN THE STATES (unless you're absolutely sure the girl is living a clean simple life). If she has to visit, go with her. Unless you're independently wealthy and can afford to give her money to send back to Brazil, she'll want to start working. With limited English and no papers yet, where is the 1st place she'll think about going. You got it . . . THE STRIP CLUB! Once some of these girls find out how much other girls make in the sex trade . . . you're screwed!

3. Many of these girls really do just want the papers. Once they get them, many times it's . . . ADIOS! Unless you . . . (refer to #4 & #6)

4. If your libido isn't up to par, you better get those blue pills. The majority of Brasilieras I know love sex and if you're not doing the job. . . . . .

5. Keep tabs and don't give too much freedom (at least in the beginning) to go off by herself (or not calling in to check up on her). Once again, refer to #2 & #4.

6. LEARN THE LANGUAGE! You will meet SO MANY MORE Brazilian women if you can even basically commuicate [*sic*] with them and you will tend to keep them longer (never mind the fact that you will be able to understand what she's talking about on the phone). . . .

Good luck in finding your ideal woman brothers![29]

While many of my colleagues in second language acquisition studies cringe at such utilitarian approaches to language learning, as a professor of French studies, I can in principle appreciate *bgcaliber1*'s emphatic suggestion to learn the Portuguese language, despite the suggestion's questionable context. But that context necessarily feeds into the myth that these ethereal beauties, these "ideal wom[e]n," are sex goddesses to boot. They require constant monitoring for fear of cuckolding, are predisposed to work in the sex entertainment industry, and require flaccid-penised paramours to come with a prescription of Viagra. In the Brazilian woman, the African American male has met his sexual match—at least in these scripts of sexual insatiability penned by African American men. Better still, with all this talk of Viagra, the African American male, that quintessential cocksman, "the keeper of the impalpable gate," in Fanon speak, "that opens into the realm of orgies, of bacchanals, of delirious sexual sensations,"[30] has been bested by *Brasilieras*.

That the mania over Brazil has reached an interesting pitch is bizarrely revealed by a certain John Nicholson who claims to be an associate of pioneering filmmaker Warrington Hudlin, whose box office draws *Boomerang* and *House Party* helped to establish hip hop film as a subgenre of American cinema. Nicholson wants African American men on the African American Men & Brazilian Women message board to provide him and Hudlin insight into their Brazil connections as they are purportedly making a documentary on Brazil, much to the chagrin of many of the men who frequent the site:

This is John Nicholson, and i [*sic*] would like to address what appears to be some growing concerns expressed by some of the men about the motives and results of the documentary Warrington Hudlin and I are working on about african american men who love/enjoy the women in brasil. First, my 100% goal is to present a very fair and unbiased look at the entire situation on Rio. I have zero interest in making a T&A (tits and ass) documentary, this will be a serious and fair look at Rio.

Now some have expressed concerns that i am interested in doing this documentary at all. I and Warrington feel that its a compelling and interesting story to be told. Some have said that they prefer if we did not complete the documentary at [all], for fear that too many people will find out and ruin a "good thing." I think its fair to say that after Snoops [*sic*] music video, if it was a secret before, it certainly is not one now.

Men need to keep in mind, that the talk about Brasil is spreading in the african american community, and while my goal is to do a fair look at this issue, there may be others who might simply want to make a one sided and sensational type piece, that would not be fair and balanced. Maybe some show like Oprah will eventually send down a production team with hidden camera's and mics and blow brothers out the water with the video.

Which is why its important to me that i complete this project and get it out there as soon as i can. I will gladly answers any concerns, issues or questions any of you may have, please feel free to email me at JNicholson30339@yahoo.com.[31]

What is most telling about Nicholson's posting is the exclusive reference to Rio de Janeiro, his use of "or," signaled by the slash between "love/enjoy," rather than "and" in reference to loving "or" enjoying Brazilian women, and the "good thing" his documentary will ruin—sexual paradise spoiled by a sea of competing African American males. African American men have choices. They can "love" Brazilian women, as many of them genuinely do, but *Brasilieras* can also be merely enjoyed, sampled like exotic victuals as *ChgoBachelor31_4U* suggests, depending on "if your [*sic*] there (1) week . . . (10 females) . . . (2) (20 females)." Indeed, the sheer number of Brazilian female dishes available depending on one's travel schedule rather resembles a colonial Indonesian rice table in which the wealthy colonists selected the finest and most succulent dishes from the isles of Asia.

The exclusive mention of Rio tells yet another story. The Avocet T&E-Varig deal to Bahia is targeted to African American females between the ages of twenty-five and fifty-five, seeking a more spiritual vacation. The first imported enslaved Africans arrived in Salvador, Bahia in the sixteenth century. Bahia and northern Brazil represent the stronghold of African culture with the ever-present martial-art school teaching the Angolan-inspired Capoeira and Yoruban-derived spiritual practices such as Candomblé. Though sex tourism is a persistent problem in Salvador da Bahia and the North, and the Bahian Carnival is also ballyhooed on sex tourist sites like Brazilmensclub.com as such a celebration that "every man owes it to himself to go once in his life," Rio becomes the exclusive playground for African American male sexual prerogatives. And the arrest of twenty-nine African American men on charges of sexual tourism with forty Brazilian sex workers (*garota de programa,* also known as GDP) on the schooner *Shangrilá,* leaving the Marina da Glòria in Rio on June 11, 2005, demonstrates the exercising of those prerogatives. It is then not particularly surprising that Rio, the *favelas,* and the women are varyingly put to use in hip hop culture.

With "Beautiful," "Why You Wanna," *Dude: We're Going to Rio,* and "Holla, Holla" videos, Snoop, T.I., Pharrell, and Ja Rule not only represented the mobility, influence, and access to affluence available to African American hip hop generation men as part of our new global condition, but also offered up the latest fetishized commodity of beauty in the heterosexual African American male realm of desire. That the "Eye Candy" section of hip hop magazines like *XXL* and the Dirty South's *Ozone* feature video vixens remarkably similar to the women in "Beautiful" is no coincidence. That we seem to see the "same ho[s]," using Tupac's rancid poetic maneuver, in Brazil, in *XXL,* and in hip hop videos in general is unfortunately a conundrum of the new black gender politics that uses art, technological innovation, and globalization in the service of color chauvinism, sexist exploitation, and hair neurosis. It is a new black gender politics completely in the service of a jack-legged black masculinity. And that black masculinity has been cobbled together from the stultifying remains of white supremacy, media, and the undeserved privileges accrued globally by American manhood.

That young black women continue to negotiate these impossible ideals that literally gyrate around them in videos, assail them from above in Madison Avenue billboards, and stare back at them in mainstream and hip hop magazines in myriad ways is nothing new. We have always attempted to carve spaces for ourselves in an American culture that has resolutely tried to deny our very humanity and womanhood. But the spaces that have emerged in commercial hip hop are categorically one-dimensional. Beauty is nothing short of the helpmate to sex; and we have become reducible to our sexuality as the predominate arbiter of our reality. Into this rotten stew of hypersexuality and insatiability, one can add the distressing outcome of sexual abuse—of which young black women and girls are 10 percent more likely to be survivors.

TOO HOT TO BE BOTHERED

Black Women and Sexual Abuse

[W]e, black women, have always been supportive
of black men in the struggle against racism, even
while we were being raped. Even while rape and
assault has been going on in our communities.
This is important because so many react as if
talking about rape and assault in our communities is somehow not being supportive of black
men, or as if it were not being loyal to black men.
　　—AISHAH SHAHIDAH SIMMONS,
　　　　Independent Filmmaker[1]

The larger question is, "What transpires in our
community that allows such a thing to be on the
minds of young men who are six and seven years
old?"
　　—CREG WILLIAMS, former superintendent
　　　　of the St. Louis Public Schools, in
　　　　response to the sexual assault of a
　　　　second-grader by twelve of her peers
　　　　in spring 2006 at a school playground
　　　　during recess

"Have you seen the tape?" a
rather smart female student inquired of the R. Kelly tape.
"That was him! And that was obviously a very young girl.
She had to ask him for sexual directives!" But no sooner
than I had proceeded to lecture about interstate trafficking

of child pornography (we were in New York, the R. Kelly tape was made in Illinois), another sex tape surfaced featuring Louisiana rapper Mystikal. These Jive Record label mates obviously had a predilection for video recording their peccadilloes. Whether those peccadilloes are more accurately described as consensual pornography or plain old sexual abuse continues to be debated in the court of public opinion. And the mainstreaming of hip hop has broadened the umbrella under which male celebrities, specifically, can seek and acquire protection from allegations of sexual violence. Industry movers and shakers, legal eagles, hip hop magazines, blogs, a multiracial fan base, and sundry artists rise to the occasion with the result being the minimalization of the crimes (reduced sentencing plea deals) and the further demoralization of the survivors who become tagged as groupies, hoochies, and chickenheads.

While it is undeniable that blacks have been used in various ways to further our national dialogues on sex and violence, sociological and crime studies have found that young women, regardless of race, are more likely to be raped or sexually assaulted and young black women are least likely to report such violence. The usual racial defensiveness or protectiveness of black communities minimizes the negative impact of sexual violence within black communities, especially when the perpetrator is a celebrity.

Feminism helped to politicize rape, which has led to legislation such as the Violence Against Women Act of 1998 and rape shield laws, which funded programs to address domestic violence and sexual abuse and disallowed probing into women's past sexual histories in rape cases, respectively.

Rape shield statutes were invoked during *Mike Gerard Tyson v. The State of Indiana* and challenged in *The State of Colorado v. Kobe Bean Bryant.* Feminists' treatises on rape have historically led to interesting developments around the issue of black-on-black rape and the protectiveness of black communities. In the nineteenth century, the history of black male lynching on trumped-up charges of interracial rape were referred to as "southern horrors" by feminist Ida B. Wells in her withering newspaper editorials and pamphlets.[2] Almost a century later in the 1970s, feminist tracts such as Susan Brownmiller's popular book *Against Our Will* presented highly problematic treatments of Emmett Till and the interracial sexual abuse of black women. In their respective eras, and with salient resonance even today, both contributed to the racial defensiveness of African American communities. Each in their own way ironically contributes to the erasure of black women's sexual abuse by black men.

In efforts to distance themselves from the "paranoia" and overbearing "victim" status conferred on women by feminism, hip hop generation feminist writers like Katie Roiphe (*The Morning After: Sex, Fear and Feminism*) reject the notion that we live in a "rape culture." According to Roiphe:

> As I see it, there are more than two sides to any issue. . . . The image that emerges from feminist preoccupations with rape and sexual harassment is that of women as victims, offended by a professor's dirty joke, verbally pressured into sex by peers. This image of a delicate woman bears a striking resemblance to that fifties ideal my mother and the other women of her generation fought so hard to get away from. They didn't like her passivity, her wide-eyed innocence. They didn't like the fact that she was perpetually offended by

sexual innuendo. . . . they worked and marched, shouted and wrote, to make her irrelevant to their daughters. But here she is again, with her pure intentions and her wide-eyes. Only this time it is the feminists themselves who are breathing life into her.[3]

Roiphe's impatience with these "retrograde" tendencies in feminism, especially on college campuses, relates to its insistence on conferring victim status on women and the culture of fear into which she sees feminism breathing new life. Instead of liberating women, Roiphe sees feminism as painting women into a corner of passivity and fear. Criticism of American culture as a whole as fear-ridden and danger-obsessed has also been taken up in Barry Glassner's book *The Culture of Fear: Why Americans Are Afraid of the Wrong Things*. Glassner's thesis was featured, particularly with respect to black males, in filmmaker Michael Moore's *Bowling for Columbine*. In his book, Glassner explains how poignant anecdotes are often substituted for scientific evidence; he demonstrates how pundits with little to no background on various social, political, or economic issues are routinely transformed into experts. Incidents that in most other cultures would invite no more than a passing reference become trends of this or that social or moral failing. Where Glassner's analyses would incite from Roiphe an enthusiastic, "Here, here!" would certainly be his unpacking of cultural stereotypes of groups of people (men) writ large as innately dangerous. Feminist's efforts to tackle sexual abuse via "Take Back the Night" vigils, educational literature, workshops, and seminars are read by Roiphe and others as part of the fear-inciting trends endemic in American culture.

But quite different from the boy who cried wolf only to have his third call ignored when the wolf actually appeared, sexual abuse in the United States statistically occurs with odds greater than one in three.[4] Research on historic under-reporting by institutions, from the military to universities and colleges, and by those who experience sexual abuse bear this out.[5] And women's organizations committed to sexual abuse education on college campuses must balance an institution's desire to present itself as a safe place for female coeds and their own missions to inform young women about sex, safety, and numbers that oftentimes vastly differ from the official institutional count of sexual assaults. Indeed, on my very own campus, by the fifth week of school in fall 2005, eighteen sexual assaults had occurred and were reported to the Women's Center, though only twelve had been reported to university authorities. Silence, shame, and secrecy are pervasive. Women's organizations, for all of our stereotyped yelping and victim-status-seeking antics, as Roiphe would have it, provide potentially sex life altering services.

As much as we would like to wish away sexual abuse in our body politic and sexual politics, that 61 percent of instances of sexual violence go unreported, that black women are 10 percent more likely to be victimized than all other women, that 90 percent of sexual assaults and rapes are intraracial, that white men represent 52 percent of rapists despite the black male boogeyman in the white imagination, that perpetrators of violence against black women serve less time than perpetrators of violence against white and Latina women, that 94 percent (or 15 out 16) of rapists will never spend a day in prison, compels hip hop generationers to seriously engage the issue.[6] If we can, and we should, revel proudly in hip hop's influence in spheres from fashion to lexicon, then the overtly sexual and sexist nature of much of hip hop culture also suggests its guidance on matters of sex.

While statistics on sexual assault and rape are crucial in this context, just as important to explore is how hip hop generationers interpret sexual abuse, and how women in particular perceive the perpetrators of this abuse. In this chapter, I explore the relationship between hip hop culture and sexual abuse. In what ways does hip hop culture ride shotgun in a culture already rife with sexual abuse? How does this culture reinforce stereotypes of black women as "so hot" that they are rendered fair game for rape and sexual assault? As I explore these questions, I draw from various high-profile cases and hip hop generation films including *Michael "Mystikal" Tyler v. The State of Louisiana, The State of Colorado v. Kobe Bean Bryant, Robert R. Kelly v. The State of Illinois,* and Ice Cube's *The Player's Club* and Aishah Shahidah Simmon's rape documentary *NO!* to further tease out issues of consent, hip hop generation gender politics, and sexual violence.

*   *   *

Hip hop culture is no more or less violent and sexist than other American cultural products (think *Playboy,* prime-time news and television, the flourishing Hooters restaurant chain and now-bankrupt airline, *The O'Reilly Factor,* hard rock, country music, the blues, or Abercrombie and Fitch catalogues). However, it is more dubiously highlighted by the media as the source of violent misogyny in American youth culture. But this is really not the point. As gifted an MC as DMX is, the lyrics to "X Is Coming" ("If you gotta daughter older than fifteen, Ima rape her") deeply disturb, as do Tupac Shakur's "First let my nigga fuck then I fuck / That's how we do it (ha, ha)," NWA's "One Less Bitch" ("I was thinking the worst but yo I had to let my niggaz fuck her first yeah / Loaded up the 44 yo, then I straight smoked the ho"), which fantasizes about the gang rape and snuffing of a woman, or the forced abortion suggested by hip hop artist Joe Budden in the remix of Usher's "Confessions" ("If she's talkin' 'bout keepin' it / One hit to the stomach, she's leakin' it"). Even if one dismisses outright causal relationship theories (rap glorifies and thereby sanctions and leads to sexual abuse, etc.), the urban, ghetto (sur)reality that hip hop artists claim to be merely describing or fantasizing about—pulling trains, forced abortions, and rape—offers a rather forlorn snapshot of young black women's sexual experiences.

Dr. Dre's very public 1991 physical beat-down of Dee Barnes, former host of the *Pump It Up* rap show, at a party provided the earliest glimpse into the kinds of brutality directed at black women for "getting out of pocket" by their hip hop generation male peers. Barnes had incurred Dre's wrath because she allowed former NWA member Ice Cube to deliver a verbal slap at NWA on her show. Gender violence directed at black women was not new. Criticisms of rap music's misogyny were also not new. But no one was prepared for the very visceral display of what many had concluded was hip hop generation men's emerging worldview vis-à-vis black women, that is, in borrowing those fateful seven words from Kanye West, "Black men don't care about black women." That one of the tracks from the Ying Yang Twin's *United States of Atlanta* could be jokingly referred to as the "date rape song" or "porn on record," comparing its lewdness to the seductive talk of Barry White by DJ Smurf in an interview in *XXL* magazine, is unsettling for a number of reasons. The inability to distinguish seduction from rape and the high frequency of acquaintance rape are two that come to mind.[7] Indeed, DMX's autobiography, *E.A.R.L.: The Autobiography of DMX*, refers disparagingly to his casual sexual partners as "dirty bitches" and "rats," as in "hood rats," with whom he had trysts on project rooftops, in stairwells, and in parks.[8] When women are reduced to a sort of *species rodentia* any matter of treatment goes.

NWA's and DMX's lyrics are perhaps more aptly described as sexually violent fantasies or more specifically, as Robin D. G. Kelly relates, "snuff [porn]."[9] And yet the frequent occurrence of Tupac Shakur–style sex trains are certainly corroborated by the chilling narratives in Tricia's Rose's *Longing to Tell: Black Women Talk About Sexuality and Intimacy* as well as the Motivational Educational Entertainment study, *This Is My Reality: The Price of Sex*. And artists are no longer content with just rapping about their pornographic lifestyles. From the blog *The Porning Report* to *The New York Times*, many have noted hip hop culture's crossover into the $11 billion pornographic film industry with grand marquee names such as Mystikal's *Liquid City*, Snoop Dogg's *Buckwild Bus Tour, Doggystyle*, and *Diary of a Pimp*, G-Unit's *Groupie Love*, Luther "Uncle Luke" Campbell's *Best of Luke's Freakshows*, volumes 1–6, and Lil' Jon and the Eastside Boyz's *American Sex Series*. Pornography is often associated with visual pleasure—magazines, celluloid, and the Web—but the sexual and sometimes violent misogyny offered up by hip hop music provides aural pleasure. The lyrical stimuli of "The Whisper Song," with its refrain, "Wait till you see my dick, I'mma beat that pussy up," appear straight out of a phone sex junky's repertoire. That male hip hop generationers have also transformed the porn industry is not especially surprising given hip hop's penetration into every aspect of American commerce. Hip hop's varyingly sexually violent misogyny, encased in "bitch-ho-pimp" gender politics, has been superimposed onto an already raunchily perceived industry. According to University of California, Santa Barbara, Women's Studies professor Mireille Miller-Young, who researches black women sex workers in pornography, this evolving gender politics has made it increasingly difficult for the black women professionals in the porn industry.[10]

2 Live Crew's *As Nasty as They Want to Be* first sparked the national debate about hip hop culture as a purveyor of aural and visual pornographic pleasure. The release of the 1989 album immediately fanned the flames of an ongoing battle over the government's authority in dictating what constitutes obscenity and what citizens should listen to, watch, and read. As a prelude to the court case brought on appeal in Broward County, Florida, state prosecutors charged an owner of a record store with obscenity for selling *As Nasty as They Wanna Be*. In June 1990 conservative lawyer Jim Thompson convinced a federal district judge to declare the rap group's third album, which contained the chart-topping "Me So Horny," legally obscene. Two days after the ruling,

the group performed songs from the album live at a night-club in Broward County, complete with booty-shaking dancers; they were subsequently arrested.

The ensuing trial hosted a cast of personages that included public intellectual and distinguished Harvard University professor Henry Louis Gates, who was then a professor of English at Duke University. With his notable book *The Signifying Monkey: A Theory of African American Literary Criticism,* which described signifying as part of the black vernacular tradition, Gates proceeded to parse the linguistic merits of 2 Live Crew's lewd puns and sexual braggadocio and rap music's claim as art. The defense queried whether the use of "four letter words" detracted from rap's being considered an art form. As a defense witness, Gates responded that, "The greatest literary tradition in English literature . . . people such as Chaucer and Shakespeare, Greek literature, Western literature, has always in its vernacular . . . included a lot of lewdity, a lot of verbal puns, sexual puns, curse words, etc."[11]

Playing a barely audible tape of the concerts at various moments during trial, the prosecution in its turn recited at length the group's lyrics from the album: "I will be fucking you / you will be sucking me then licking my asshole; lick it 'til your tongue turns doodoo brown." In cross-examining Professor Gates, the prosecutor asked, "[T]hat's great classical literature?" Gates offered the rejoinder: "I never said it was Shakespeare."[12] The obscenity ruling was overturned on appeal. And the trial in fact greatly bolstered album sales. *As Nasty as They Wanna Be* went on to move more than three million units. Though trial jurors requested permission from the presiding judge to laugh at the recital of various lyrics, we have now finally come to understand that 2 Live Crew's lyrical antics were no laughing matter.

Ahead of the curve and in response to the 2 Live Crew obscenity hullabaloo and Gates's defense of such rap as art and signifying, writer and law professor Kimberlé Crenshaw suggests in an editorial appearing in the *Boston Review,* "Beyond Racism and Misogyny: Black Feminism and 2 Live Crew," that this variety of aural pleasure is

> no mere braggadocio. Those of us who are concerned about the high rates of gender violence in our communities must be troubled by the possible connections between these images and tolerance for violence against women. Children and teenagers are listening to this music, and I am concerned that the range of acceptable behavior is being broadened by the constant propagation of anti-women imagery. I'm concerned, too, about young Black women who, like young men, are learning that their value lies between their legs. Unlike men, however, their sexual value is a depletable commodity; by expending it, girls become whores and boys become men.[13]

Crenshaw's "concerns," while raised almost fifteen years ago, still have relevance today. In these male-spun "raps of passage" or "*bildungsrap,*" black women's bodies are prefigured as accessible, exchangeable, and expendable. Discussions—academic, fictionalized, and pedestrian—have given us plenty of insight and opinions into the historical exploitation and misrepresentations of black female sexuality. From nineteenth-century black women activists to historians Darlene Clark Hine and Nell Painter to writers Toni Morrison and Akiba Solomon, black women have explored every facet of the twin myths of hypersexuality and easy accessibility that emerged in the New World as part and parcel of black women's initiation into what it meant to be chattel.

In post-antebellum America, black and white men antagonistically retreated to their separate corners over charges of interracial rape, with vows to protect their respective communities and women. Black males, first as slaves and then as freedmen, were far less able to conform to American patriarchal rituals and rites of protection. And the focus on interracial rape allowed a peculiar silence to reign with respect to women's sexual lives within both communities. Where black women raised the issue of intraracial sexual abuse, particularly if publicly, as in the 1970s–1980s fiction of Toni Morrison, Alice Walker, Ntozake Shange, and countless others, the level of vitriol was intense.

The maturation of hip hop and its generation of writers and thinkers are confronted with a very different, highly complicated world regarding gender and racial politics, linked explicitly to feminism and the civil rights and black nationalist movements. Given the historical backdrop of chattel slavery and sexual violence and the overarching puritanical obsessions of American culture, a respectability yoked to sexual conservatism emerged in post-antebellum America. While explicitly linked to the middle class, it became the overarching code dominating black conduct irrespective of class and despite stereotypes and myths of black disrepute. In matters of sex, relations deemed respectable were always within a heterosexual and preferably marital and monogamous framework.

While the sexual and racial liberalism wrought by the

women's and black rights efforts pried open white women's knees and loosened black men's belts, on the whole, black women continued to struggle against ungenerous characterizations of their moral and sexual integrity. Like their foremothers of the late-nineteenth- and twentieth-century Black Women's Club movement, respectability still offered the surest path toward safeguarding their integrity.

The ethos of sexual liberalism nonetheless permeated the stranglehold sexual puritanism maintained on American culture. The generation following second wave feminism and civil rights and black power era struggles, the hip hop generation, experiences sexual innuendo in the most mundane of consumer activities and banter. Hip hop culture's sexual expressivity is a marked contrast to the old-guard code of respectable sexual conduct, and thereby holds itself out as freedom (even if it is a mere perversion of freedom), a release. Young black women are torn between the politics of respectability and a bizarre version of "sexual liberation." Disseminated by an omnipresent media culture, this distorted vision of sexual freedom is built upon the age-old twin myths—of hypersexuality and easy accessibility—against which so many young women continue to struggle.

The new transracial dialogue surrounding hip hop culture also advances the visual, aural, and physical traffic in women—all women, regardless of race. The gains made by movement mommas and pappas have equally allowed women the autonomy to decide whether or not they will participate in such consumption-oriented sexual trafficking. Despite the "multiculti" mantra of hip hop pundits and the multinational corporate interests that have much at stake in such rhetorical marketing, black women's bodies continue to be the primary free-floating signifier of sex showcased in hip hop for multiracial and transnational consumption. The sad irony about the notion of "choice" and "autonomy" for us black women who choose to appropriate and project the twin myths whether as rap artists, "video ho's," or Jane Does (perhaps "Jainnye Doe," for we black women would never spell our names so—well—plainly), is that the choice is never fully ours, and thus, the sexual freedom is illusory. Hip hop's corporate formula for female desirability includes large helpings of the crudest manifestations of supposed male desires that reproduce the twin myths. Black women's sexuality in the marketplace of hip hop—in this instance, the supine or prostrate variety—is then devalued and heavily discounted.

Interestingly, in an era when intraracial sexual abuse can be systematically documented as alarming, where black women are aurally (music) and visually (music videos, hip hop porn, and hip hop films) molested, our coordinated responses and efforts have not even received the same vitriolic reception or coverage from black men as Michelle Wallace's *Black Macho and the Myth of the Superwoman,* Walker's *The Color Purple,* and Shange's *For Colored Girls* generated during the black power era. Incendiary reviews, name calling, and ostracism from the *Black Scholar* to the *Black Collegian* came down like a deluge on these black women writers. These rabid responses helped to legitimize black women's studies and black feminist criticism, and opened the door for black women writers. Our concerns about the sexually violent misogyny of hip hop culture or artists in

particular have been generally fobbed off in such a way as to
generate more inflammatory materials for public consumption and therefore colluding media coverage, press junkets,
and more billions of dollars in CD and DVD sales. A vivid
example is Tupac Shakur's open letter to the late activist C.
Delores Tucker in response to her highly publicized national
campaign about the demeaning treatment of black women
in hip hop. In his ditty, "Wonda Why They Call U Bitch,"
Shakur attempts to justify why some women are "bitches."
He mocks Tucker by explaining: "Figured you wanted to
know / why we call them hos bitches / and maybe this might
help you understand."[14] Critiques of sexual abuse in hip hop
by black women seem to invite more pugilism—physical and
lyrical. It is not so much that we don't count. We do—in obviously various insidious ways. But we also in truth do not
add up to too much—certainly not more than the profits to
be had at our expense.

These perversions of desirability set young black women
up as "too hot to be bothered," so accommodating sexually
that that bothersome word, "No!" has no place in our rep-
ertoire. In effect, it would appear that in our own communities black women are viewed as not sexually assailable unless we are trespassed by white male interlopers (as was the
case with the alleged interracial rape of Tawana Brawley
that riveted the nation and mobilized black communities
with Reverend Al Sharpton at the helm). Conversely, we are
ostracized (Desiree Washington, Ayanna Jackson) within our
communities if the accused is a well-known black male
(Mike Tyson, Tupac Shakur). But the vast majority of young
black women who have been sexually assaulted end up as

piles upon piles of anonymous bodies relegated to a scrap heap of unprosecuted and unsolved crimes. This scrap heap allows the practices of sexual abuse to continue with near legal impunity, thereby dangerously reinforcing the idea that sexual violence is not a pressing issue among hip hop generationers. Rather unemployment, law enforcement malfeasance, black male-on-male violence, black men on the down-low, and the HIV/AIDS pandemic *are* the paramount issues. Hence, frenzied public debates about culpability rage on, regardless of the damning, and growing, bodies of evidence— from vaginal lacerations to tearful testimonies, from pubescent flesh to all of those pornographic videotapes.

*   *   *

Despite a long history of sexual misconduct, the repeatedly "saved," as in spiritually redeemed, multi-talented R&B/gospel and hip hop collaborating hit-maker R. Kelly allegedly mocked before a mostly female audience the pending criminal charges against him at the September 29, 2004, Chicago kickoff of the disastrous "The Best of Both Worlds" tour with rapper Jay-Z. And he does have a record: four settled lawsuits of sexual harassment, one twelve-count child pornography case in Polk County, Florida, dropped in 2003 because of prosecutorial misconduct involving an exploratory search and seizure warrant, a 2005 pending civil suit by a woman who alleges hip hop generationer Kelly taped their sex interlude and distributed it widely on the Internet without her consent, and one 2002 pending case of fourteen counts of possession of child pornography stemming from a twenty-nine-minute home-recorded video. Jim DeRogatis, a reporter who has been doggedly following the *Robert R. Kelly vs. The State of Illinois* case, documented Kelly's concert in an article entitled "R. Kelly Flouting His Foes." According to Kelly's attorneys, DeRogatis "is so focused on Kelly's criminal case that he sees it everywhere—even in places it is not."[15]

DeRogatis's allegations stemmed from a number of concert antics that included: a skit involving young women in orange prison gear in a simulated jail cell, an e-mail message displayed on a concert screen requesting a female companion at least nineteen or over, and, the decisive stroke, flowing yellow water on the stage as a backdrop (several of the sexual charges against Kelly involve urination). DeRogatis is perhaps not the best at semiotics, as the yellow flowing water is a reference to "Honey Love" from Kelly's 1991 *Born into the 90s* album. He is also probably not the most objective. He is a witness for the prosecution. And R. Kelly, who has pled not guilty, is of course innocent until proven guilty, and absolutely free to exercise his first amendment rights as his lawyers contend. But as African American journalist Mary Mitchell perhaps too pithily argues, Kelly is "the poster child for the dysfunctional relationship that has developed between adult men and girls in our society."[16]

Kelly's "devil-may-care" attitude might stem in no small way from his millions of albums sold, the number two *Billboard* debut of 2004's *Happy People/U Saved Me,* the number one *Billboard* debut of 2005's *TP3 Reloaded* with five hundred thousand units moved in three days, the urban popularity of his five-part ballad "Trapped in the Closet," the repeated requests for collaborations from artists as varied as

Britney Spears and Celine Dion, the calls to write music for Broadway, and the invitation to perform from the Congressional Black Caucus.[17] The highlight of Kelly's raffish attitude can literally be seen on the Spring 2004 cover of *XXL* magazine, where a pimped-out Kelly is dubbed the "Teflon Don."[18] Like the New York crime boss John Gotti's evasion of federal prosecution thoughout the 1980s, Kelly has been thus far able to escape repeated attempts by prosecutors to make criminal charges stick to him.

The specter of race in such matters of sex, however, cannot help but rear its untoward head. That Kelly à la Mitchell would become "the poster boy" for illicit sex with underage girls reeks of a sort of bizarre cultural whitewash and knee-jerk journalistic response that works, inadvertently in Mitchell's case, to buttress stereotypical ideas regarding black male and female sexuality.

Our Lolita-obsessed culture is neither the invention nor the exclusive domain of blacks. R. Kelly's media turn as Vladimir Nabokov's Humbert Humbert and Clare Quilty of the hip hop generation reminds me of the ways in which blacks, in this case, black males, predictably become poster boys for sexual impropriety in America's high-stakes battles over morality and (white) innocence. For example: Tupac Shakur and Mike Tyson become synonymous with our exorcising of demons over date rape rather than William Kennedy Smith, a well-known serial date rapist who media pundits concluded was an "unlikely candidate for the rapist's role";[19] Clarence Thomas with sexual harassment rather than serial harasser Senator Robert Packwood; O. J. Simpson with domestic violence rather than all-star baseball player Steve

Garvey; Michael Jackson with child molestation rather than the droves of devout Catholic priests; the Indiana Pacers trio of Ron Artest, Jermaine O'Neal, and Stephen Jackson with violence in sports rather than the slew of assaults in the (mostly white) National Hockey League against other players and fans.

Hyperbole aside, the fact of the matter is that R. Kelly is not the "poster child for the dysfunction between adult men and girls." Rather the public's wishy-washiness—at times "shocked and awed" then shushed by a beat-laced Kelly lullaby—epitomizes, as Mary Mitchell rightly concludes in this instance, that "most of us don't give a darn about the sexual exploitation of [black] girls," or women for that matter. And a good number of those to be counted among that "most of us" who don't give a darn are black women—those avid purchasers of Kelly concert tickets and albums, and continuing participants in Kelly-orchestrated sexcapades.

In an interesting twist in the tale of the tape, Dirty South platinum-rapper Mystikal's foray into homemade porn helped land him a six-year prison term on reduced charges of sexual battery of the infirmed on January 15, 2004. The "infirmed" in this case suggested that (1) "the victim is incapable of resisting or of understanding the nature of the act by reason of stupor or abnormal condition of the mind produced by an intoxicating, narcotic, or anesthetic agent administered by or with the privity of the offender; (2) The victim has such incapacity, by reason of a stupor or abnormal condition of mind from any cause, and the offender knew or should have known of the victim's incapacity."[20] While Kelly's lawyers have assiduously denied that the male participant in the tape is Kelly, throwing a sideways glance to Kelly's brother as well as forcing the prosecution to pin down the fifty-one-month window in which the sex acts allegedly occurred, Michael "Mystikal" Tyler could neither deny his presence on the tape nor his participation in the premeditated sex acts on his hairstylist. Angered that his longtime friend and hairstylist cashed un-authorized checks from his account upward of $80,000, he forced the woman to perform oral sex; he then invited two male acquaintances over to rape and sodomize her. Portions of the interlude were video-recorded for posterity, or, as defense attorney J. David Bourland would later argue, to prove that the interlude was consensual.[21]

Prosecutors added extortion to the charge, for the rapper effectively extorted sex from the woman by asking her to do something "degrading"[22] in exchange for his not pressing charges against her for theft. While Mystikal's attorneys attempted to finagle a signed affidavit of consensual sex from the woman to buttress his original claim of innocence, the discovery of the tape by the police in a safe at Mystikal's Baton Rouge, Louisiana apartment forced the rapper into a plea agreement. The original charges of aggravated rape and extortion, respectively carrying a mandatory life sentence and up to fifteen years, were bartered down to sexual battery of the infirmed, which carried the possibility of probation. The rapper underwent sexual assault counseling and performed community service. He, and his record label, also arranged for monetary compensation for the woman and anticipated, like the other 94 percent of sexual abusers, that he would never spend a day in prison.

Despite the fact that the prosecution and the defense had agreed to keep the videotape sealed and not submit it into evidence in the case, Judge Anthony Marabella asked to view the tape prior to sentencing. The tape was of such an inflammatory nature that the judge concluded that the woman had been "terrorized" and that Mystikal believed "he was above the law and can take the law into his own hands."[23] Judge Marbella could have sentenced the rapper to the maximum ten-year term. He instead sentenced him to six years with eligibility for parole in 2006, and five years probation for extortion. Marbella closed by further admonishing the rapper, "You received a significant break when the district attorney reduced the charges. . . . If it weren't for the victim, the sentence would have been the maximum 10 years."[24] The rape survivor effectively offered Mystikal a reprieve by accepting the terms of the plea agreement. Prosecution of the rapper on the original "aggravated rape" charge would have allowed that "inflammatory" tape to become part of the public record.

That Mystikal believed that rape is "just deserts" for theft rings out loudly during an interview with *Sister2Sister* publisher Jamie Foster Brown. All the while proclaiming "genuine love" for the woman (one shudders in thinking about the punishment meted out to those he does not hold dear), when asked what would he do if he could do it all over again, he says, "Probably what I did—or something real close to it."[25] The rapper accuses the hairstylist of breaking "his trust" and offers ersatz solidarity with rape victims: "They're getting swept kicked. Their feet are getting swept under. This is a direct blow to them. You just don't do that.

Especially, the person that is accusing me of it. Y'all can't fathom how painful that is."[26]

That there is something painfully disturbing about Mystikal's revelations with respect to sexual violence, masculinity, power, and loyalty is an understatement. Restitution of the ill-gotten funds and termination (surely there were scores of hairdressers to be had in Baton Rouge) were not even on the table. Hip hop's "keep it real, keep it street" codes of conduct, regardless of women's desires to abide by them and own them, are highly male-centric and regulated, and so women are often casualties in their complicity.

Take Lil' Kim, who was sentenced to serve a year and a day for lying under oath to protect her former label mates (these same label mates repaid her in kind by turning state's evidence and trying to profit from the trial proceedings). In her last interview before turning herself over to authorities to serve her time, Kim offers: "Unfortunately, me as a woman, I had to take one for the team, and when I say for the team I say hip hop, because I was the poster child for the federal government, for their investigations."[27] While there might be some truth to Kimberly Jones's attempts to cast her lot in a grand narrative of prosecutorial overzealousness and a government crackdown on hip hop (the same claims could certainly be made about the maven of domesticity Martha Stewart as a celebrity poster child for insider trading), what is closer to the truth is that she took one for the hip hop team composed predominantly of men admittedly undeserving of such sacrifice.

In hip hop generation gender politics, women's transgressions are often met with verbal, sexual, or physical assault.

This übermasculine ethos is governed by its own makeshift rules, as the "po-po" (police) or legal system has proven itself ineffective at best and antagonistic and untrustworthy at worst. Hip hop is not a culture of violence. American culture, however, thrives on aggression. Violence, when deemed necessary, is seen as a viable alternative, one that has been sanctioned, institutionalized, and unilaterally practiced in the United States, from the hang-'em-high foreign and domestic policies of the Bush administration to the sexual assaults in the Abu Ghraib prison as a way to interrogate and terrorize prisoners to the bombings of U.S. abortion clinics. Violence in hip hop is a manifestation (and an easy scapegoat) for a much more prevalent American violence that much of (white) America would rather ignore. Despite the fact that young black men like Mystikal have multiplatinum-selling albums that guarantee them a life outside a ghetto reality, they prefer to stay connected to the street culture whose invaluable lessons and *realness* have allowed them to earn their bread and butter as "authentic" hip hop artists. In effect, the hairstylist took Mystikal's "*shit,*" his money, what was his, and he took in return what was undeniably hers. It is clear from his various interviews that he felt personally and understandably violated; in delivering his version of street justice—a gendered street justice—he violates her publicly by not only sharing her violation with his entourage but by taping the incident.

Borrowing from feminist lawyer and anti-pornographer campaigner Catharine MacKinnon's charge that writer Carlin Romano publicly raped her on the printed page,[28] writer Tanya Horeck, in her book *Public Rape,* argues that sexual violence on film is indeed a form of "public rape."[29] A private violation that usually occurs between victim and victimizer(s), scenes of sexual abuse and rape in films invite public participation—whether they are offered up for interpretation in courtrooms, courts of public opinion, or screened at home in designated media rooms among one's boys. In the case of Mystikal and Kelly, the taped sexual acts continue to be debated as proof of guilt in courtrooms *and* courts of public opinion despite Mystikal's conviction. Indeed, Mystikal's attorney argued that while the videotape "evaporated their opportunity to go to trial . . . it was not done for any voyeur-type purposes. It was done because [Tyler] didn't want there to be a misunderstanding. . . . But Michael wanted it to be a record that he wasn't trying to make someone do something beyond their will."[30] The subtleties of coercion, and the bartering of sex for perceived transgressions of loyalty, seem lost on the defense attorney and the rapper. Given the defense's fight to keep the tape out of court and the way Mystikal's secretly stowed the tape in a safe and never offered it as corroborative evidence, Bourland's assertion regarding the tape's corroborative nature begs the questions: A record for whom? And who exactly would need to view the tape to determine that there was no malfeasance involved? If the sex acts were indeed consensual why make a tape at all? After all it *was* the *tape* that corroborated the sex acts and led to Mystikal's imprisonment.

* * *

While many hip hop stars have been counseled by old school hustlers, pimps, and stars to tape sex acts to disprove false charges of rape, it would appear that Mystikal intended the tape for other purposes—blackmail/extortion, or merely future viewing pleasure. In truth, the Mystikal "sex, lies, and videotape" debacle and R. Kelly's turn as sex taskmaster on film to underage girls are nothing more than homespun porn, which depicts black women and sexual abuse on the order of Ice Cube's *Player's Club* (1998) and Joe Esterhaz and Paul Voerhoven's *Showgirls* (1995).

In some respects *Player's Club,* Cube's directorial debut, is the black answer to *Showgirls.* Both films are morality tales that conclude with rape scenes: "bad things happen to nice girls who hang out with the glamorized strippers that are Vegas showgirls" and "bad things happen to naïve girls who become strippers." Esterhaz's rape scene, where a black woman is gang raped to the battle call "Fresh Pussy" has been proclaimed "over the top" (when is rape ever *not* over the top?) by the late film critic Gene Siskel. Similarly, the online reviewer for *celebritywonder.com* suggests that Cube's "unsure directorial skills" did not provide enough "buildup" to his film's rape scene, which could have rendered it "exponentially more harrowing." Rape is indeed a spectator sport, when some viewers prefer it less "over the top," while others require a "buildup."

The Player's Club is neither poorly written, nor directed, nor acted. As the black version of *Showgirls* only better—better casting, better acting, better script—*Player's Club,* coming three years after *Showgirls,* attempts to right some of *Showgirls*'s wrongs by explicitly addressing the issues of sexual violence, race, gender, class, and power. Though *Showgirls*'s heroine, Nomi, beats the wealthy white male celebrity (that lethal combination of audacious privilege) rapist silly, he will never do a day's time in jail for his orchestrated gang rape of the film's moral center, a collegiate black seamstress. In contrast, the working-class, clownish, and patently dull (as in not too bright) rapist and his stereotyped predatory lesbian sister in *The Player's Club* will do deserved time in what have become young black men and women's homes away from home: prison. Unlike *Showgirls,* the show will not go on at *The Player's Club.* At movie's end, the ill-fated club is ceremoniously torched. And in the wake of its smoke and rubble go young men's fantasies and dollars and young women's hopes and dreams of easier money and lives.

The wrongs seem to be righted in *The Player's Club*'s denouement: Junior and Ronni are carted off for jail; the shady "Dollar Bill," played by Bernie Mac, is disappeared by the loan shark St. Louis and his henchmen; Diana/Diamond graduates college, and Ebony is a reformed stripper dispensing unsolicited counsels and trading barbs with sharp-tongued shake dancers between selling them shoes. However, the rape scene in *The Player's Club* troubles, and not because of Cube's "unsure directorial skills" that precluded "a buildup" necessary to convey the "harrowing" act that rape is. Indeed it is the buildup to the rape that disturbs because it touches upon the very crux of the dilemma regarding the sexual abuse of black women and black male complicity via their participatory silence in the abuse.

Miffed that a few nights earlier he and his partner were unable to "pull a train" on the inebriated Ebony (played wonderfully by Monica Calhoun) due to her cousin's (Diamond/Diana) cock blocking, Clyde (Ice Cube) re-approaches

Ebony at Junior's bachelor's party. Her arrival has been eagerly anticipated by the assembled men, who in the meantime had been bonding over pornographic videos. The now-sober Ebony unceremoniously tells him, "No! motherfucker, No! Don't you know what 'No' means?" Ice Cube's character does an interesting take on the feminist "Take Back the Night" battle cry against sexual violence: "No means No!" and Clyde sets up the dimwitted Junior by telling him that Ebony will "let him fuck her." Like a snake-oil salesman he then gives Junior a condom and tells him to inform Ebony that he and his partner understand "that 'No! means No!'" Like sexual voyeurs, the other male partygoers wait outside of the door listening passively to cries, slaps, screams, and lamps crashing. Rather than stop the rape, they shake their heads in mutual disgust and leave.

The response is quite reminiscent of that of Tupac Shakur, whose unwillingness to intervene in the assault of his female companion Ayanna Jackson by his associates landed him in Rikers. When asked by Kevin Powell in an April 1995 interview with *Vibe* why he did not intervene, Shakur revealed that male camaraderie superseded his intervention, "How do I look saying, 'hold on'? That would be like I'm making her my girl." As the men bonded over the pornographic films awaiting Ebony's arrival, they too bonded silently over her rape—in disgust and shameless lack of intervention.

The politics of respectability and the protection of womanhood has been thoroughly replaced in black youth culture by variations of male bonding found prominently in an "it ain't no fun if my homies can't have none" mentality. But every now and then, there may be a break in the male ranks on the order of hip hop generation sports icon Kobe Bryant. Many black men were willing to stand empathetically with Bryant in solidarity against Colorado native Katelyn Faber's allegation of rape, despite the media's attempts early in his career to set him apart as a smarter, multilingual loner, who usually listened to hip hop via headphones after practice. Bryant was cast as a man apart from the supposed rogue-ridden, outlaw culture of the predominantly black NBA. Overnight, Bryant fell from his lofty perch amidst the hailstorm of tarnishing news media comparisons with the Othello-like Jack Johnson and O. J Simpson. Black men, all too familiar with white America's fleeting paeans to the race-transcending black male athlete, offered Bryant shelter. However, when investigators' interviews revealed that Bryant stated that his former teammate Shaquille O'Neal dealt with "bimbo eruptions" with payoffs, a male chorus could be heard chanting variations of: "Weak, Weak, Weak!" Bryant had broken the ranks of male privilege and silence regarding sexual assault. His self-serving, hand-caught-in-the-till revelation of O'Neal's philandering and payoffs shed some light equally on the sex and gender dynamics in the realm of sports among, in critic Todd Boyd's words, "the young, black, rich, and famous." After all, charges of sexual abuse are fairly common.

Despite Katelyn Faber's varied semen-specimen-stained panties, Bryant's predilection for ejaculating on women's faces while allegedly asking, "Do you like it when a black (m-f) comes on your face?"[31] and, according to *Denver7 News* legal analyst Craig Silverman, the defense's "nut (as in mental instability) and slut" theories, what is especially troubling is that the word "No!" and consent, more specifically, seem to be a high-stakes game of interpretation. "No!" may be clearly articulated, as in the fictionalized rape of Ebony in *The Player's Club*; it can be maliciously understood by Ice Cube's Clyde; it may also prove a source of befuddlement as was the case with the detectives in the Bryant trial who questioned why Faber never clearly told Bryant, "No!"[32] Similarly, consent may be coerced as in the case of Mystikal's hairstylist, or incapable of being given from the legal standpoint of age, as in the R. Kelly case. But what is evidently clear is that in each of these instances, the responsibility for male sexual impropriety seems to fall squarely to hip hop generation women.

*   *   *

It comes as no surprise that hip hop generation independent filmmaker Aishah Simmons's documentary *NO!* about rape and silence offers up hip hop videos featuring gyrating scantily clad women between clips from *Fallen Champ: The Untold Story of Mike Tyson* of a National Baptist Convention support rally for Mike Tyson (amid charges of rape and deviant sexual conduct) and Minister Louis Farrakhan's berating of women regarding, "How many times . . . have you said, 'no,' and you meant, 'Yes?'" Over soy-laced caffeinated drinks and hot chocolate at Nashville's Bongo Java, Simmons explains:

> These lyrics . . . recent footage of "Tip Drill," perpetuates the myth of black women wanting, willing, able and asking for what they get. I used the images [hip hop videos] in the context of sexual violence. We see it as entertainment. I want to challenge these images in the context of women talking about their experiences of sexual violence.[33]

NO! then presents the varied ways that black women are forced to carry the responsibility for male sexual impropriety in a global culture that accrues billions of dollars by objectifying them.

Simmons's documentary suggests that there is a direct correlation between the sexual abuse of black women and the visual culture that objectifies black women as sexually available. The stereotyping nature of visual media informs hip hop generationers' sexual politics. Taken as a whole, Simmons's film seems to propose that the stereotype of sexual availability in hip hop provides a bridge to all other verbal and physically exploitive acts. In this argument Simmons builds upon an idea stated most powerfully by Catharine MacKinnon regarding public violation. And to further expand our understanding of sexual abuse in the black community, *NO!* does not dabble long in the straightforward (in terms of legal adjudication) condemnable act of stranger rape, with only one of the women's narratives recounting a stranger rape. Rather, Simmons takes us into the more complex and frequently occurring realm of acquaintance rape.

Blending narratives of trauma by black women, archival footage, historical recreations, and commentaries from a cadre of both female and male scholars and community activists, the film challenges us to confront head on the issue of rape and sexual assault by black men (and boys) in black communities. Questioning the silence surrounding sexualized gender violence, Simmons reveals that she decided to make the film in response to the silence of communities at large and the black community in particular. Acknowledging her own status as a survivor of sexual violence, she also relates that her mother, featured in *NO!*, is also a survivor. "Why are we silent when so many women and girls are affected by this?" Simmons asks in exasperation. The audience then understands immediately that the women featured in the film are no longer silent, as Simmons uses each of the women's voices in one scene simultaneously. We hear words like "my rapist," "I refused to give him," and others. That Simmons has author Charlotte Pierce-Baker read from her courageous book *Surviving the Silence* hammers home the importance of giving voice to the trauma and its impact on women's lives and the communities within which they live.

But perhaps one of the most telling moments in *NO!*, which brings us back to the issue of consent and the "aggressor-take-all" interpretation of the word "No!" is the simple but stark revelation of rape activist John T. Dickerson, Jr., of Bluegrass Rape Crisis Center. Dickerson states that, "Men can stop rape if they want." In the matter of acquaintance sexual abuse, communication on matters of sex between hip hop generationers is imperative. Accepting that "no means no," despite elder Minister Farrakhan's willy-nilly "no-means-yes-damned-deceitful-games-you-play"[34] counsels about black women, could go a long way toward edifying our generation's most intimate interactions.

But sadly, black men are not going to suddenly wake up one morning with a new understanding of "No." The larger and more difficult question is, If men can stop sexual abuse, why wouldn't they want to? And as the former superintendent of the St. Louis Public Schools queried, What is transpiring in our communities that would sanction such jarring behavior? Truth be told, too much of our culture—both hip hop culture and American culture at large—gives men and boys every reason to continue gender violence. How to counteract such behavior is at the crux of the hip hop generation's dilemma. Statistics on the sexual abuse of black women and girls tell only part of the story. Interventions like *NO!* and poignant stories of sexual abuse like those laid bare by black women in *Surviving the Silence* and *Longing to Tell* move us toward understanding the exacting costs of rape to communities (mistrust, crippling fear), despite black women's personal narratives of resiliency. Such interventions reveal rape as not an act of lust or sexual desire, but a violent crime motivated by the desire to punish, humiliate, or dominate. They reveal the sexual abuse of black women and girls as a betrayal of community. Male sexual coercion—of the nagging, persistent, "Please, baby, please" sort, or the threatening violent variety—leading up to female acquiescence does not add up to consent. What we need then is to continue the dialogue in earnest about how hip hop generation men and women understand sexual abuse as it relates to culpability, responsibility, and that gnarled concept, at least when it comes to matters of sex, of respect.

"I'M A HUSTLA, BABY"

Groupie Love and the Hip Hop Star

Tonight you wanna fuck with me its
   alright with me
Come on an gimme that groupie love
            —G-Unit, "Groupie Love," *Beg for Mercy*

You ain't no better cuz you don't be
   fucking rappers
You only fuck with actors, you still getting
   fucked backwards . . .
            —Jay-Z, "Bitches & Sistas," *The Blueprint 2:*
            The Gift & The Curse

very generation of artists
has its followers and fans. However, groupies are a world
apart. And with the increasing popularity of hip hop and the
coarsening of mainstream taste manifested by the public's
tolerance for sexist obscenity and misogynist pornography
on wax marketed as entertainment, what used to be clan-
destine sexual activities reserved for backstage, hotel, or lim-
ousine chatter has become exhibitionist male fodder for a
voyeuristic public. Along with the video vixen whose curvy
silhouette can command as much as three thousand dollars
per video appearance (e.g., Esther of Petey Pablo's "Freek-
A-Leek"),[1] inspire internet forums and threads, and *Vibe*
music award categories ("Sexiest Video Vixen"—Ki Toy for

OutKast's "I Like the Way You Move"), there are strip club dancers whose fancy foot, butt, and pole work inform an entire generation of young women and tantalize generations of men. Hip hop groupies and the sexual favors they dispense —thanks to the wagging tongues of male hip hop artists— have also been catapulted into the limelight.

Not since the 1960s–1970s rock scene have groupies been so cavalierly feted and lyrically flogged. Rock music's groupie following, while predominantly white, did include black groupies. Emmaretta Marks, a Rolling Stones favorite, and one-monikered women like Winona and Devon—Jimi Hendrix's muse for the song "Dolly Dagger"—are just a few well-known rock-era black groupies. The Rolling Stones' song "Brown Sugar" clearly rejoices in more than the granulated substance found in most kitchen cupboards. And Sir Michael "Mick" Jagger's liaisons with *Hair* actress and former groupie Marsha Hunt (the result of which was daughter Karis Jagger) are testaments made flesh to the words, "(a-ha) brown sugar how come you taste so good / just like a just like a black girl should." While black groupies could be found here and there in rock culture, hip hop enjoys an even broader multiethnic groupie base with a palette of variously shaped and hued black women holding down more than their fair share of that base.

The word "groupie" made its first appearance in the American lexicon in the 1960s. *Rolling Stone* magazine celebrated the groupie in its February 1969 issue. And, the spate of mainstream film releases on groupie culture and rock music—*The Banger Sisters* and Cameron Crowe's *Almost Famous,* with its groupie entourage humorously referred to as the "Band-Aids"—attests to the prevalence of groupie mania in that era. When rock groupie Pamela Des Barres penned her experiences in *I'm With the Band: Confessions of a Groupie* (1987) (a volume that has gone through several reprintings), her coming-of-age rock memoir became the first insider account of rock groupie culture.[2] Candid in its revelations about drug abuse, depression, sex, and her naïve disappointment with feckless rock stars, Des Barres portrays rock-era groupies as a celebrated yet ragtag lot. Des Barres's groupies become cast, at least in her narrative, as muse-like characters on the music scene, setting the social pace and even going as far as creating their own groupie rock band, the GTOs, under the tutelage of the venerable Frank Zappa. Nonetheless Des Barres's rosy spin on her turn as a groupie is punctuated with a good deal of deep knee bending and head bobbing, which speaks to the hard-and-fast purpose of groupies of her era and beyond. While the romanticized stuff of films, songs, magazine articles, and memoirs, rock-era groupies were an undeniably stigmatized collection of women whose use-value directly corresponded with their sexual liberalism.

In hip hop culture, groupies are often referred to as "bitches," "hoochies," "chickenheads," "golddiggers," "ho's," "tricks," and "skeezas," although some would argue that hip hop artists are not as discriminating in their tossing out of derogatory terms for women. Groupies are not mere autograph seekers, avid fans, or loyal followers. Groupies are intimacy aspirants who vicariously derive power or fame (however small) from knowing public men privately.

The relationship between hip hop celebrities and groupies, however, is a tenuous one. The sheer number of rap tracks that riff on groupies reveals the symbiotic relationship between groupies and rappers. While disparaged, dismissed, and perennially "fucked backwards," in the words of Jay-Z, the presence of groupies is integral to safeguarding a seemingly fragile masculinity that is heavily contingent upon female acquiescence and accessibility. In an era where women are rapidly scaling the education and socioeconomic ladders, where on average college-educated black males earn less than men from every other ethnic group (and a mere $3,900 more annually than college-educated black women),[3] and where policing and prisons exert in great disparity social authority over poor and working-class black men's lives, the bedroom, at once a private space, has become a public one via music videos, porn flicks, and music tracks. In this space, the mythic dominance of black men and their perfected craft of "dicksmithing" appear uncontested by all, irrespective of race, class, and gender.

In general, groupies authenticate the hip hop star's successful cultivation of his craft, his flow, his game, which is thoroughly part and parcel of his selfhood. Groupies may be handy, interchangeable, throwaway women, but they are also ego-intoxicating and self-affirming for hip hop stars. They sexually bear witness to the extraordinariness of men who without a microphone, corporate office at Bad Boy Entertainment or Def Jam Records, a New Line Cinema picture deal, nimble crossover or lay-up, or enviable batting or rushing average would be otherwise quite ordinary.

Hip hop groupie mania, that is, male artists' desire for seemingly uncomplicated and submissive "groupie love," and women's conspicuously pruned and preened eagerness to be serviceable, replicates in some respects traditional gender roles. Hip hop groupies trade on their bottoms, or less pointedly, their femininity as measured by their sexual desirability. Hip hop generation men's masculinity and desirability is weighted on material accoutrements as measured by a "bling" lifestyle or a chart-topping record.[4] And also, the bargain struck in hip hop groupie culture, though, stokes a visceral misogyny informed by existing American gender relations. Like racism, sexism and misogyny are not mere aberrations in an otherwise healthy U.S. body politic; they are thoroughly necessary to the functioning of our equality-loving-but-hard-pressed-to-fully-realize democracy.[5] Sexism and misogyny are grist for the patriarchal mill.

The scorn heaped upon groupies by hip hop stars is therefore tied to a keen awareness that the bargain is flimflam, just one in a series of stereotypical feminine betrayals that reveal the artist's "extraordinariness" as transient as the groupie. In other words, the extraordinariness of the hip hop star lasts about as long as it takes for the next someone famous to come along. As rapper Killer Mike insightfully puts it: "[W]ith a groupie, it ain't about you. It's about her. She's just fulfilling her moment. You're just a character in the story. Tomorrow it's gonna be Nelly and then it'll be Young Buck."[6]

Whether the groupie is an occasional or transient one who procures intimacy as opportunities present themselves, or a committed one who pursues with single-mindedness certain hip hop artists, the cynicism inspired by groupies is in truth the recognition that groupie mania is just as much a hustle as the rap game, the basketball game, the strip game, the Hollywood game, the academic game, and so forth. Hip hop groupies are collectors of those perceived as rich, famous, and powerful. The operative word here is "perceived" because many hip hop stars have signed shoddy, exploitive deals or are cash-poor because of consumption-laden lifestyles. Hip hop stars may *sex* them but groupies hustle and *collect* them[7] like baseball cards, trading up for the next prized card. And with each card and trade, there is always a story behind the acquisition. Hence, the rules of engagement in the "pimps up, draws down"[8] bargain involves sexing and kicking groupies unceremoniously to the curb in order to avoid "catching feelings"; using protection because groupies get around; a rather homophobic/homoerotic precaution regarding never kissing a groupie on the mouth given the lore around their knee-bending proclivities (for one could figuratively be sucking another man's penis); and never parting with hard-earned dollars lest one be labeled a "mark," "busta," or worse, a "Captain Save a Hoe"—rapper E-40's panegyric to the golddigger's ideal man. But despite hip hop's rules of engagement vis-à-vis groupies, the reality suggests that hip hop stars are sparing with the truth —at least according to the "Groupie Confessions" published in *Ozone* magazine and Karrine "Superhead" Steffans's *Confessions of a Video Vixen.*

You see I had this brother who was mad at me
Some of y'all be foolin' us
Big feet big hands just plain big
The sex ain't worth a damn
We women wanna know these things
If y'all got the bat but not the swang.

—TLC, "Girl Talk," *3D*

When the "Groupie Confessions" appeared in *Ozone* magazine, a kerfuffle quickly ensued. A relatively new addition (May 2002) in a growing field of southern-based independent hip hop magazines that include *Tha Hole, Holla, Rude,* and *Block2Block, Ozone* magazine proclaims itself to be the "Southern Voice of Hip-Hop Music." While the Bronx may be the birthplace of U.S. hip hop culture, Atlanta, Miami, Memphis, New Orleans, and mid-southern cities such as St. Louis and Nashville have nurtured the talents of artists like Master P, Ludacris, OutKast, the Ying Yang Twins, Lil' Jon, T.I., Young Buck, Jacki-O, Chingy, Nelly, and Trina. Many of these artists have developed distinctive styles with crunk, drawling inflections, and a southern lingua franca to become some of the most heavily rotated artists on cable network video programming and commercial radio. Atlanta native T.I.'s Best Male Hip-Hop Artist win at the 2006 BET Awards clearly signals the mercurial rise of the south.

Ozone also has the noteworthy distinction of having as its publisher and editor-in-chief Julia Beverly, an entrepreneurial young white woman. Inspired by *The Source, Vibe,* and *XXL,* Beverly took her camera, dollars, and dreams and developed *Ozone.*[9] Some higher-brow publications like *The New York Post* have called the magazine "ghetto fried," as in steeped deep in ghetto culture. And Beverly's editorial vision for *Ozone* may drive some to curse the democratization of publishing via inexpensive desktop systems; yet, the service to the southern hip hop industry that the magazine provides garnered the publication an Urban Magazine of the Year award at the Southern Entertainment Awards in Nashville in February 2005. The magazine is also rapidly expanding—securing a contract with a national distributor in February 2006.

The first installment of the "Groupie Confessions" was published in the magazine's second annual sex issue. A stroke of pure marketing genius, the buzz generated by the confessions led to increased subscriptions, dozens of on-air readings from Florida, where the magazine is based, to Wendy Williams at WBLS in New York, articles in *The Philadelphia Daily News* and *The New York Post,* thirty thousand downloads from *Ozone*'s Web site, and the ire of both Method Man's wife as well as Jay-Z's publicist.[10] In an industry saturated with groupie tales, Beverly pursued the "confessions of groupies" because she wanted to know "what was in it for them." As the *Ozone* editor-in-chief contends, "The thing is none of the people we interviewed would describe themselves as a 'groupie.' For a lot of people, sex is power. Sex is a huge part of hip hop, but since it's such a male-dominated field you are rarely hearing both sides of the story. I wanted to get the women's perspective."[11]

Though not especially methodical for those purists of data collection, Beverly circulated her research interests in hip hop quarters, or in hip hop vernacular, "put the word out on the street" and set up a call-in system that blocked numbers for the women to detail their most intimate interludes with hip hop stars. Beverly then sorted through the stories selecting the most "credible" and "intriguing" (read: salacious). Like a literary version of *BET Uncut,* some of the interviews are graphic and read like the stuff in Bob Guccionne's *Penthouse* forums. As the editor notes, because the interviews were anonymous, authenticating the groupie tales was impossible. And yet one can never fully verify the truth-fulness of such intimate matters without the highly unlikely express corroboration of the hip hop star involved (think: the patently false denials of DMX regarding paternity of two children, despite DNA test confirmation). And who, given the unflattering details of some of the confessions, would admit to such dismal sexual exploits? Like the messiness of sorting through the "he did"/"she said, 'No!'" of date or acquaintance rape in the absence of physical evidence, credi-bility and an admission of sexual contact by the alleged of-fending party are vital. In the end, sides will be taken, with most settling on some version of the cliché: "No one really knows the truth but those two people."

Intriguing still is that the anonymity of the interviews obscures the race of the groupies. The method of collec-tion, "putting the word out on the streets," the equivalent of what writer Zora Neale Hurston called the "black dis-patch," allows a bit of leeway in terms of inferring that the serialized "Groupie Confessions" has netted more than one black hip hop groupie. In fact, one woman self-identified as white (May 2005) and only two women self-identified as black; both admissions were in the context of revealing a ce-lebrity's predilection for white (Tyrese) and lighter-skinned black women (Lil' Wayne). Certainly one could infer that even in the context of "groupie love" a hierarchy is present —that "thinner, blonder, lighter" women are preferred.[12] Preference and predilections may have their place, but trysts with groupies are more like "catch as catch can" affairs; availability and willingness, whatever the color or race of the woman, take precedence.

The truth is black hip hop groupies are a deliberately secretive bunch, hence buttonholing them into face-to-face interviews is nearly impossible. Even Julia Beverly had to forgo her idea of the groupie story for the first sex issue of *Ozone* because no one would talk until she changed her method of interviewing. And in a telephone conversation with Des Barres about her forthcoming book, *Let's Spend the Night Together: Backstage Secrets, Rock Muses, and Super Groupies,* in which she attempts to include hip hop groupies or "modern girls," as she calls them, she similarly related hitting a near wall of silence. The exception was a woman who told of her encounters with Dr. Dre, but nobody was giving up information on hip hop's honorary black white boy, the elusive Eminem, despite rapper 50 Cent's reference to Eminem's alter ego "Slim Shady" in "Groupie Love." The other adjustment Des Barres made to her second project revolved around the book's title. She "had to add *'muses'* because unlike the classic groupies many of the modern girls don't consider themselves groupies."[13]

Part of the hip hop groupie hustle is relative anonymity (to all but the hip hop star circuit) and secrecy. Being marked as a serial groupie who blabs incessantly about her exploits would greatly diminish future opportunities for collecting hip hop stars, particularly in the era of HIV/AIDS where, according to the Center for Disease Control, hip hop generation black women represent 67 percent of all new HIV/AIDS cases.[14] The celebrity, albeit abased, associated with groupies that began during the 1960s–1970s, has not carried over into the era of hip hop. Very few women today would publicly claim the mantle of groupie as it is mired in the freakiest of sexual innuendos and the worst stereotypes of female manipulation and scheming, thanks in large part to the scathing lyrical characterizations by hip hop artists.

While groupies of all ethnicities have always served as payola for male accomplishments in various arenas—from the sanctity of the church pulpit to the basketball courts—their presence was always a shadowy one until they exploded on the rock scene. Des Barres's generation of groupies benefited from the interesting and propitious collision of second-wave feminism and rock music, which created a much-hyped scene for sexual experimentation, particularly among (white) women. There is little to be gained by "coming out" publicly as a black female hip hop generation groupie. Black women have always been painted with the broad brush of sexual accessibility and avarice. In effect, the sexual freedom bestowed upon the radicals of the 1960s is one that black women have been culturally and socially stigmatized as already having and purposefully pursuing.

The exception to this anonymity, secrecy, and the gains to be had is Karrine Steffans, whose *Confessions of a Video Vixen* could have just as appropriately been titled *Confessions of a Hip Hop Groupie*. As it stands, the current title does a disservice to the many women who legitimately work in the hip hop video industry with agency representation. Steffans's video vixen appearances were nothing short of pick-up games—a means of short-term employment and access to hip hop stars. Even Steffans earnestly acknowledges in an interview with *Essence*'s Teresa Wilitz that the other video models were "totally different from me. I was the only person as far out as I was."[15] The book's title demonstrates, as *Ozone* publisher Julia Beverly related, that even "group-ies" don't want to be identified as such. And the rancor, contempt, and abuse to which Steffans has been subjected, from blogs to interviews with Tyra Banks, the Queen of Dice, and Slice and Mix-It Up, Wendy Williams, Miss Jones @ Hot 97, and Star and Buc Wild at 105.1, all but assures that the shroud of secrecy and virtual silence around hip hop groupie mania will remain neatly in tact.

In the tradition of shock radio, the Miss Jones Show @ Hot 97 had already run into controversy with "USA for Indonesia," referred to popularly as the "Tsunami Song." Satirizing the crisis and its victims, the lyrics ran afoul of any semblance of political correctness:

Knowing other kids
There was a time when the sun was shining bright
So I went down to the beach to catch me a tan
Then the next thing I knew a wave 20 feet high
Came and washed your country away
And all at once you could hear the screaming chinks
And no one was safe from the wave
There were Africans drowning
Little Chinamen swept away
You could hear God laughing, "Swim you bitches, swim!"
So now you're screwed
It's the Tsunami
You better run or kiss your ass away
Go find your mommy I just saw go by
A tree went through her head
And now your children will be sold to child slavery.

With calls for the firing or suspension of Jones and her co-hosts as well as demands that sponsors pull advertisements, the controversy eventually morphed into a discussion of black xenophobia and anti-Asian racism. Squaring off with Miss Info (DJ Minya Oh), the Asian American counterpart on the morning show who found the song woefully short of humor, Jones and crew were forced to donate a token portion of their salaries to help the crisis victims. The song also cost Emmis Communications, the show's parent company, losses in advertising revenue and two employees. While Jones and her crew claimed political correctness, their Howard Stern antics were especially hard to swallow given blacks' own painful history of slavery, the undeniable existence of child sex slavery rings in Asia, and the race and poverty-riddled after-effects of New Orleans's Hurricane Katrina.

On the heels of the "Tsunami Song" uproar, on July 7, 2005, Steffans appeared on Miss Jones's Hot 97 show, in an interview that careened out of control. Even for those who absolutely cannot truck with Steffans's "suck-and-tell" memoir, the leering and jeering commentary appeared intended to further grind Steffans into degraded oblivion. No matter how one may view Steffans's sexcapades, her book resonates with a telling number of black women readers. As a result, examining what led Steffans to live the groupie life would have been perhaps a useful and instructive topic for journalistic investigation.

But the Hot 97 show was anything but. In between Steffans's attempts to answer questions, the host interjected barbs like, "This just in, more whoring," and commentaries about her "nice ass," and the front flap of the book's dust jacket where a come-hither photo of Steffans begs for elicit virile responses to the contours of her female anatomy. To Steffans's reiteration that she is no longer in the groupie hustle, the retort, "So I shouldn't solicit you for sex today," was tossed out as an Iago-like aside. With each helping of "ho" and "slut," Steffans steadfastly continued to do what she was ostensibly there to do—blithely hawk her book as a therapeutic morality tale. In the midst of the interview, Steffans abruptly exited with heels clacking in the background only to return moments later (after all books need selling).

She was then ambushed by an on-air telephone call from former "husband"/lover/pimp Kool G. Rap and his "wife" Ma Barker. The Queens-bred "Kool Genius of Rap" Nathaniel Wilson had his heyday in the late 1980s as a member of Marley Marl's Juice Crew. By the mid- to late 1990s, his three solo albums garnered neither critical nor commercial success. Considered a revered "old schooler" by the time Steffans encountered him, he allegedly Ike-Turnered her on a basis regular and on general principle during their stormy two-year relationship.

The violence-strewn state of hip hop generation interpersonal relationships, embodied by the collision between hip hop vixen Steffans and rapper Wilson and uncovered in greater journalistic detail by Elizabeth Mendez Berry in a *Vibe* article, "Love Hurts: Rap's Black Eye,"[16] is sadly publicly overshadowed by racier details of sex peddling and purchasing. That Steffans had to cancel a book signing at Hue-Man Bookstore and Café in Harlem because she feared for her safety from people both *unrelated* and related to the numerous stars she exposes provides more cud for us to chew over. That she is somehow solely burdened with the responsibility of destroying "happy homes" and devastating "innocent children" rather than the men she pleasured reeks of a double standard. Like black women victims of sexual abuse who are called upon to keep silent about intraracial sexual violence in black communities, Steffans is castigated because she detailed the seedy and subpar sexcapades of the hip hop industry: a "barking," "growling" DMX; the pompous but average performance of Sean Combs, whose attorney sent a letter to her publisher HarperCollins; the self-serving Jay-Z, who asked her to recount her wretched history with Kool G. Rap, only to request fellatio but wisely with a condom; the serial philanderer and sexually "messy" (in Steffans's words) Bobby Brown; the dwarfish, very married Ja Rule; and the experience of having to run Dr. Dre's resume and status "through [her] head" to become aroused.

A seemingly clearer-headed Steffans writes,

> I was hanging out with hip hop's elite and enjoying the best restaurants, had access to any club or party and wore the hottest fashions. . . . I became a hustler of sorts—bouncing in and out of strip clubs and selling myself in every way. I had gotten to a very desperate point where I could only have sex if it was accompanied by perks. I expected and received money from every man in my life, especially celebrities. I used sex to keep them happy and when they were happy they were generous. . . . Plus I'll be honest. I was good at using sex to get what I wanted and needed. That's all I knew.[17]

Steffans's arsenal included sex, intimacy, and pleasure as purchasable commodities; her forte was as a consummate hustler and chameleon. She morphed into whatever version of sex kitten those celebrities (and non-celebrities frequenting the various strip clubs where she worked) required. Whether she obliged sexual demands in ecstasy-laced stupors or allowed herself to be loaned out by Irv Gotti, as sex purveyor extraordinaire, everyone had to pay.

And when the payments stopped, when she hit a low point of homelessness—living out of her car with her son—they would pay some more, she decided, and this time with their reputations to the purported tune of a $7.3 million book advance. As Steffans recalls during the Hot 97 interview:

> I was everybody's best thing until I had problems. When I hit rock bottom. . . . Once I was homeless, the same person who would have written me a $10,000 check before was like, "No!" In my head, I was like, "Yeah. Okay. I got you. I'm watching you. Don't worry about it." I just always felt like one day all of this is going to make sense and you're going to be calling me. I'm getting calls now.

Indicative of our fascination with sex, celebrity, and hip hop culture, Steffans's alleged book deal exceeded that of former President Bill Clinton, though we too chomped at the bit anticipating his version of the Monica Lewinsky debacle—an affair of "cigars are for pussies" and presidential semen for blue Gap clothing store dresses. Hip hop rule-breaker that she is, Steffans detailed her trysts for money, and offered a "take that" to those who turned their backs on her after years of slavish sexual accommodation—both undeniable "no-no's" in groupie culture. Hot 97 DJ Minya Oh sums it up, "In rap there is an *omertà*, a code of silence. You do your dirt, everyone knows you do your dirt, but no one talks about it. [Karrine Steffans has] violated that code and chosen to talk about everything."[18]

As with all tell-alls, there are bound to be those "innocents" swept into the fray of conjecture. Two casualties of the *Confessions* were rappers Method Man and Big Tigger, former host of BET's *Rap City: The Bassment.* Neither is mentioned in Steffans's book. Kool G. Rap's latest paramour Ma Barker had seemingly become a confidant of Steffans. During the Hot 97 free-for-all, Barker, hell bent on discrediting Steffans, stated that Steffans told her she knew both rappers intimately. Barker also played on-air a telephone message left on her and Kool G. Rap's voicemail by Steffans. In the message, Steffans offers profuse "thank you's" to the pair for purchasing clothing for her son (Kool G. is the child's father). In Barker's kitchen-sink drama, these "thank you's" were evidence of the hip hop vixen's "false claims" about her violence-ridden past with the rapper.

With his wife's foot still deeply lodged in his behind over revelations regarding his predilections for "spank[ing]" and "hit[ting] it from the back while he pulls your hair"[19] a mere nine months earlier in *Ozone* magazine's November 2004 "Groupie Confessions," Method Man too made an impromptu appearance on the Miss Jones Show. He was implicated by Barker as the father of a second child whose existence Steffans herself declined to acknowledge, and as "Papa," the married, fatherly mystery man in her published saga. An obviously pained Method Man—perhaps his wife's foot sunk several inches deeper into his backside—vehemently denied any association with Steffans.

In a culture where masculinity is filtered through a lens of heterosexuality and homophobia, despite the presence of gay rappers, despite the homoerotic nature of the male-bonding that hip hop inspires, Tigger's alleged participation in a homosexual tryst has eyes now cast askew at his involvement in an issue that disproportionately plagues black communities and hip hop generationers in particular: HIV/AIDS prevention. Aware that the stakes are quite high, Tigger went on the offensive firmly maintaining his heterosexuality in any and every venue available—Allhiphop.com, *Ozone,* and the Miss Jones Show:

> I am heterosexual. I love women. I have never engaged in any homosexual activities, and I don't like men. . . . There's nobody on this earth that could tell you that I'm even remotely homosexual. I was actually on Hot 97 this morning and I challenged Ms. Jones or anybody else who wants to challenge me to put up $100,000 against my $100,000 to take a polygraph test. And when I win, the money is gonna go towards my charity for HIV/AIDS prevention.[20]

The terms "down-low" and "on the QT" seem to have no place in Tigger's vocabulary. But he nonetheless goes on to explain his commendably responsible motivations for setting up his Washington, D.C., charity. With "one and twenty people in D.C. infected" and "25–30% of those infected" (mostly men) unaware that they are carriers, Tigger's social outreach on this issue eclipses the efforts even of many black churches in the D.C. metro area.[21]

Interestingly, Tigger is described in *Ozone* as "the person whose reputation has suffered the most,"[22] as if being homosexual is utterly damaging. But in hip hop culture it is. Fathering children with other women while married, adultery, "messy," "growling," "average" sex (everyone has an off night, right?) are all considered "what men do." However, in the homophobic-laden worldview of hip hop culture, men loving or even casually sexing (with a condom hopefully) other men in the way that hip hop stars sex groupies is neither manly nor masculine. In the end, both Method Man and Tigger suggested some variation of Snoop Dogg's "Can You Control Yo Hoe" to Kool G. Rap regarding Ma Barker's public histrionics, as this too is a testament of manliness.

But whether the "Groupie Confessions" and Karrine Steffans's *Confessions* are fanciful yarns or "confessions of dangerous minds," the airing of such prurience does give us another side of the story—the groupies' version—even if it may be pure cock-and-bull. The "Groupie Confessions" allows our hip hop fascinated, black-masculinity-obsessed culture carnal knowledge of those celebrities. The groupies, hitherto a behind-the-scenes lot, have publicly spun sexual narratives that shred the finely cultivated hip hop image of the cocksure black male. And so we bond, giggle, "ooh" and "ah" over revelations of the tattooed, deft-ball-handling Allen Iverson's "littlest, ashiest dick"; of Jay-Z's "boring" but stereotype-conforming "humongous dick"; of Jadakiss's stereotype-defying "minute man" performance.[23] We are just tickled by Nelly's "little sausage link" and daring when encouraging the swallowing of his "pimp juice," that precious seminal liquor that would perhaps, in his mind, transform the groupie into a "Positive Intellectual Motivated Person" —a P.I.M.P.[24] But at least Nelly seems to have taken a few pages out of a "consensual sex" manual as well as notes from a "how to" book on women and the much sought after orgasm. The rapper has been known to sensitively inquire, "Is it okay if I do this? Can I touch you there? . . . Do you like this? . . . Are you gonna cum? How can I make you cum?"[25] It is of course the hip hop stars themselves who have piqued our puerile interests in their bedroom gymnastics, with all their bravado and swaggering maschismo about pipe laying, "beating the pussy up," and their mudslinging about playin' and pimpin' hoochies, groupies, chickenheads, and ho's.

And even more mind-bending than the length, girth, and bland performances of the churlish cabal of male hip hop stars are the motivations articulated by the women in "Groupie Confessions." The sexcapades of groupies are generally viewed through the prism of low self-esteem. Certainly Steffans, a survivor of gross parental neglect, rape, and domestic violence, embraces this characterization writ large. In the "Groupie Confessions," the anonymous young black women's motives for their sexual choices are varied and appear, on the surface, much more complicated. The motivations are in fact strikingly similar to a 1998 scholarly study in *The Journal of Sport and Social Issues,* "Groupies and American Baseball," which examined women's motivations for pursuing ballplayers and the strategies they used to get attention.

In the sports study, groupies were as integral to the baseball landscape, the authors note, as in hip hop culture. Unlike rappers who trumpet their dalliances and disdain for groupies under looping beats, baseball players generally shun the topic publicly except for those rare exhibitionist, tell-all sports autobiographies like Jim Bouton's *Ball Four* (1971) and Wilt Chamberlain's *View from Above* (1991). The authors conducted interviews with fifteen baseball groupies.

The women pursued relationships for various reasons: "partying" with the players, "the opportunity to act out sexual fantasies in unusual or strange places," "having a pro ballplayer would be something nice to look back on and to tell her kids," or for the adventure of it.[26] As one groupie from the study waxed on in glowing terms:

> These guys represent an adventure in a safe way because you know who they are and you can go find them if you need to. Unlike just meeting a guy in a bar, a player is not going to be a guy who is going to kill you. . . . Players come slightly recommended; you know who they are. Then there is the bragging aspect—"Oh, I slept with so and so."[27]

We should note that the matter of safety is a relative one. Though the talk of safe sex is now de rigueur, its widespread practice is debatable given paternity suits, Superhead's ecstasy- and alcohol-laced tales, and Kobe Bryant's inauspicious unprotected hanky panky. The transmission of the HIV/AIDS virus to Earvin "Magic" Johnson from multiple sex encounters with unknown women, as well as to rapper Eazy-E, whose "never turn anything down but my collar" sexual politics resulted in multiple "baby mammas" and premature death from AIDS, should certainly give one pause. As well, the "it ain't no fun if the homies can't have none" mentality pervasive in the baseball study and in hip hop groupie mania culture may lead some women into situations where consensual sex with a celebrity may result in gang rape or sexual abuse (Ayanna Jackson and Tupac Shakur and company).

Most women in the "Groupie Confessions" were clearly not interested in long-term relationships but were involved with various hip hop stars because they wanted to have sex with a celebrity: "[I]f he ain't got a hit song out, what is the attraction? He just a regular nigga"; "It was more or less just for amusement"[28]; "I'm like a nigga: conquer and destroy, and it's a wrap."[29] Some wanted bragging rights, as one indicated, "[H]e was borderline famous so I figured I'd have a story to tell. . . . I'm in the music business, so that's pretty much the reason I fucked Jay [Jay-Z]. Just to say that I did."[30] Many groupies who were asked insisted that a woman shouldn't be called a groupie "just because she wants it."[31]

As opposed to the "fuck 'em and feed 'em beans" mantra extolled in rap tales, some, including Steffans, received those supposedly withheld perks such as money, diamonds, and furs in exchange for their trysts, a night in a nice hotel and breakfast in the morning. Others, like the young woman involved with Lil' Wayne, present another perspective:

> We met after a concert, several years ago. . . . He asked if I wanted to get on the bus with him. . . . I am a big fan of his. That was my main reason for wanting to get on the bus. . . . When me and him started fucking, that's when he was with Nivea. . . . But he's kind of a ladies' man about it. He wasn't trying to jump into it. He was a gentleman. He's a real respectful guy. . . . He got married, so I respect that. We talk every now and then but we don't sleep together anymore. . . . No, I wouldn't consider myself a groupie, because I wasn't doing it because of who he was. I was kinda into him as a person. I acted the same with him as I would with a regular person who's not a rapper.[32]

The relationship between Lil' Wayne and the young woman replicates the bargain of groupie mania as it falls within the scope of traditional gender relations and beauty hierarchies that still exist in black communities. The woman trades on the "light-skin" and "long hair" that Lil' Wayne prefers, and he trades on his status as a hip hop star. On the one hand, she rejects the tag "groupie" because she "wasn't doing it because of who he was." Yet, she acknowledges that she was a "big fan," that being the motivating reason for boarding his tour bus. The line between fan and groupie is not a straight one. There is one common magnetic denominator nonetheless: hip hop–star status.

In the end, it is all about that "superstar dick," in the crass words of Snoop Dogg, and this ultimately appears to separate the worldly groupie from the fan who gets caught up in a sexual situation (Desiree Washington) or casually falls into one (the anonymous young woman with Lil' Wayne), and the "golddigger" who is out to ensnare a celebrity through marriage, pregnancy, or extortion on a trumped-up rape charge (the August 1998 dismissal of fabricated charges of rape, sodomy, and false imprisonment against DMX by a stripper or the now-settled alleged 2005 shakedown of Snoop Dogg by Kylie Bell).

Groupies can be counted on not to charge rape after consensual sex unless they are mishandled (the Tupac Shakur and Ayanna Jackson fiasco). Nonetheless, the cynicism and misogyny inspired by the easy sex and the worldview that all women are potential lawsuits waiting to happen has led to the term "groupie" becoming a catchall for all women— whether they are scandalous, predatory, of easy virtue, autograph seekers, or hapless, adoring fans. That hip hop stars make no distinction whatsoever between women who want to bed them as part of their brush-with-fame hustle, those who want to hustle them for material, marital, or maternal gain, and those who simply want autographs, hems in women's sexual autonomy and bolsters gender roles that better serve male interests—Pimps Up, Ho's Down.

Contrasting the "Groupie Confessions" with the groupie revelations in the baseball study, according to the authors, baseball groupies were reluctant to talk openly about sex except in the most general of terms. And this self-censorship may be perhaps due to the interview structure and purpose: face-to-face with researchers for a scholarly outlet versus the anonymity provided by a telephone conversation for an entertainment magazine. The interviewees in the "Groupie Confessions" were shielded from judging eyes, even as they were subjected to disapproving questions like "Did you feel like a prostitute?" or "So what's your background like, sexually? I mean, some people might look at someone who sleeps around or sleeps with famous people and assume that they were raped, or abused, as a child."[33]

The women in both the sports study and the "Groupie Confessions" rejected the moniker "groupie." Indeed, "the word put out on the street" was not an explicit call for "groupies" but the even rawer call for "anyone who had fucked a famous person."[34] What is clear is that whether the women in the "Groupie Confessions" were committed or transient groupies who happily accepted the term (like Des Barres), or were rather star-struck fans, giving way to a fantasy by doing the deeds that groupies do (thus justifiably rejecting such nomenclature), or were sexually assertive or adventurous women who have, or have had, intimate relations with hip hop stars, they became designated by the public as "groupies." Case in point: Despite the women's insistence that they were not groupies, the serialized column is titled "Groupie Confessions," and the women are deemed those who fall outside the boundaries of sexual propriety.

And yet, a perverse sort of agency appears to be at play with respect to sexual freedom, identity, and choice, as indicated by the women in the "Groupie Confessions." This sense of power is, of course, challenged from many directions, namely, by the labeling of the women as "groupies" by (black male) hip hop stars, the magazine's (white female) editor, and us—the reading public. But while we may perceive their choices as indicative of misguided sexual experimentation, low self-esteem, or an effect of feminism gone awry (it was Naomi Wolf after all who also suggested that besides shunning mainstream beauty pressures we "should be shameless. Be greedy. Pursue pleasure. . . . Tolerate other women's choices. Seek out sex we want."[35]), these young women clearly see their dalliances as an intriguing variation on the rights (and rites) of female sexual passage—a feminine privilege. "I get shit done. A nigga I want, I get him done"[36] is their mantra.

The sexual caprices of these women who "have fucked a famous person" are integral to who they purport themselves to be—self-assured women who have desires and who are firmly in control of their sexuality. They are not "girls gone wild," but women who have game ("You gotta play their game and let them think they playin' you"[37])—game enough to "conquer and destroy" a hip hop star for a night, several months, or years. It's a game that plays with socially scripted gendered roles. There is celebrity worshipping and female sexual accommodation in exchange for a story to tell where the hip hop artist has a walk-on appearance. These women do the picking and choosing of their male sexual partners. And those partners, unlike the average joe, are importantly famous, or at least "borderline."

This exercising of sexual choice and opportunity stirs that dense pot of misogyny that too frequently bubbles up and splashes all over with crudeness into hip hop culture. These freewheeling sexual practices are indeed individual choices that are at once coupled with the hedonism that hip hop has come to signify and also our larger American cultural reflexes that celebrate capitalism, consumerism, and the individual over the collective. "Famously fucked" women dispense sexual favors in order to procure the capital and currency represented by the fame, power, and riches of the hip hop star; and that currency in its turn is consumed, collected, and cosseted between thighs and lips. Sex and sexual desirability become games of one-upmanship—men pimping and playing women, women stepping up their game to serve them up in kind. This is not a gender war, battle, or even a skirmish—though many of the women use terms involving warfare ("conquer and destroy")—but sex as sport, with the winners making off with ill-gotten booty (literally).

But just who those winners are is unclear. Are they women like Steffans who may profit from airing their private demons? Are they women who will have stories to tell about their sexual exploits with famous people? While each individual may stake out a claim of success, the public airing of such "wins," like the sexually racy, misogynist braggadocio of hip hop artists, amounts to losses for the next generation. The losers are the next generation of young black girls (and boys) like those in the Center for AIDS Research (CFAR) study who consume voraciously the sexual frivolity propagated by hip hop culture and implied by groupie love. The most vulnerable of these young girls are from poor, urban environments, according to the Motivational Educational Entertainment (MEE) Report, *This Is My Reality: The Price of Sex.* The report describes the current state of sexual activities among black urban youth between the ages of thirteen and twenty as "transactional," that is, "sex is something to be used and bartered."[38] Moreover, while college-educated, upwardly mobile black women are described by *The U.S. Multicultural Women Market* report as more confident and secure with themselves, the MEE report found that poor and working-class hip hop generationers from the thirteen-to-twenty-year-old demographic are significantly influenced as well by media—that they feel greatly devalued and experience high levels of "internalized low self-esteem."[39]

In these scenarios, sex simultaneously becomes one way to exert some semblance of control and power in relationships, as well as being the primary vehicle through which young women and girls experience devaluation. As the MEE Report notes:

> Males don't particularly think it's wrong to call a female a "ho," run a "train," or "hit it and quit it." It is not unheard of for group sex (or gang rape) to occur, with a young female as the victim. Males report various ways of disrespecting and devaluing females, including running "trains" or "bust

outs" (group sex) on them, dogging them, and even handing them over to their partners to "try out."[40]

And just one tragic consequence of the freewheeling new gender politics in a multitude of others that involve teen pregnancy, welfare and poverty, and self-esteem and femininity tied to cock teasing is that young black girls, along with their thirteen-to-nineteen-year-old male counterparts, represent 65 percent of reported HIV/AIDS cases among youth, despite being only 15 percent of the U.S. population.[41] This is also despite the "Rap It Up" campaign launched by BET as part of the kind of sex education needed to ensure safe and emotionally healthy sex lives for young black girls and women.

Owing principally to hip hop artists and now the women themselves, the "black groupie" has moved from the shadowy sidelines to a full-blown presence with multiple voices and a face (Steffans) in hip hop culture. The private exchanges between hip hop stars and groupies, while at the bottom a transaction of sex for celebrity, receive a public hearing via a black cultural tradition: call and response. While hip hop artists rap about the groupie, the women write and interview about them. The call curses and praises those hallowed tools of sex and beauty in the groupie arsenal. The response details how those tools open the keystone to celebrity, money, power, and perks. Whether she is silent or answers the call, whether we can verify her existence or she is merely an invention of a wanna-be hip hop player's rhapsodic rap of easy sex and scandalous schemers, the idea of the groupie is a powerful trope in hip hop culture. She is a metaphor for male sexual prowess, indeed, puffed-up black masculinity—the stuff that has become the bedrock of commercialized hip hop. She also represents the intensely transactional nature of hip hop gender dynamics.

STRIP TAILS

Booty Clappin', P-poppin', Shake Dancing

> Now pop that coochie you know the procedure
> If you want this cash gotta make that ass shake
>   like a seizure
> —LUDACRIS, "P-Poppin," *Chicken-N-Beer*

> The strippers like my music and they play my
> music in a lot of the strip clubs. . . . They travel
> and dance all over and they were taking my mu-
> sic and performing in different strip clubs in other
> cities. . . . they had something to do with my mu-
> sic getting out there.
> —KHIA, Tampa, Florida, rapper[1]

> A stripper's story may end in any number of ways,
> but the beginning rarely varies: Young woman
> needs money. Young woman casts about wildly,
> weighs options, and in some crazy moment, con-
> siders stripping. Young woman measures poten-
> tial worst-case scenario against potential pot of
> cash. Young woman steels nerves and makes leap.
> —LILY BURANA, *Strip City: A Stripper's
> Farewell Journey across America*

Magic City is a place that effortlessly marries sexual fantasy and one-stop shopping for hip hop record deals and video vixens. It is the hot spot where aspiring rappers attempt to toss their latest studio products into the hands of the likes of Jermaine Dupri, Executive Vice President of Urban Music at Virgin, rapper and Disturbing Tha Peace (DTP) collective member Ludacris, or Chairman and CEO of Island Def Jam L.A. Reid. It is also the place where those moguls and artists test market music before a highly discriminating group of dance music connoisseurs—black women in the adult entertainment industry also known as strippers, exotic dancers, and shake dancers.

Located hoofing distance from both Spelman College for women in Atlanta, Georgia, and the Greyhound bus station, in the hopes perhaps of drawing recruits from both sites with enticing offers of tuition and erectile assistance, Magic City is usually brimming with high rollers, ballers, and a parking lot jampacked with luxury vehicles and "hoopties" alike. The club has helped fill a niche left by the scandalously drummed-out-of-business Gold Club. The Gold Club was one of the most popular strip clubs in Atlanta. Frequented by celebrities, athletes, and politicians, the Gold Club put Atlanta on the map as "Southern Sex Central" despite Georgia's Bible Belt conservatism.

The hubbub surrounding the Gold Club is dutifully documented by hip hop generationer Jacklyn "Diva" Bush in her tell-all memoir *The Gold Club: The Jacklyn "Diva" Bush Story: How I Went from the Gold Room to the Court Room*. Bush danced at the Gold Club from 1997 through 2000. Thanks to lax city and state ordinances regarding serving alcohol in nude clubs, in its heyday, the Gold Club netted annually one-fifth of Atlanta's then $100 million-a-year sex industry. Indicted by the IRS and federal government for using the club as a front for prostitution, money laundering, credit card fraud, and racketeering, Jacklyn Bush is considered the black Heidi Fleiss of strip clubs, or, as she writes vividly and with a bit of hyperbole of her Gold Club days and of Atlanta's sex entertainment industry, she was "the Michael Jordan of the stripping industry":

> Some people say that I was the Michael Jordan of the strip-ping industry. Well, maybe I was. . . . I started dancing in Milwaukee at the age of 18 and ended in what was arguably the most prestigious, high-dollar, high-class strip club in the United States—the world famous Atlanta Gold Club. . . . [Atlanta] is the city where the adult entertainment industry is second only to Coca-Cola. . . . The Gold Club was a haven for men of high means, high rollers, guys who thought noth-ing of dropping a $4,000 tip. Women who thought nothing of a lesbian sex show and two well-placed fingers. GHB. Ec-stasy. Cocaine. Chicks with kids and boyfriends at home. College girls looking for an easy way to get through school.[2]

Bush describes the highly charged atmosphere of the Gold Club with its intermittent Vegas-style shows, S&M lesbian intermissions, and VIP and Gold Rooms where all sorts of activities from prostitution to Gold Club sundaes (a heady combination of dancers, male clients, whipped cream, straw-berries, chocolate syrup, and expensive champagne) were of-fered. She also provides a glimpse into the lives of the club's workers—from single moms to college students. Unlike the Gold Club, however, Magic City's dancers and clientele are predominantly black and its primary music format is bass-heavy hip hop, reggae, and R&B.

Rappers give shout outs to strip clubs like Magic City and Body Tap (Atlanta) and the Pink Slip (Brooklyn, Illinois) in much of the same way they give props to their 'hoods

(Cashville/Nashville, north Memphis, Brooklyn), designer drugs and alcohol ('X" and "Cris"), and criminal offenses ("187"). In a January 4, 2004, interview with Dave DiMartino at Yahoo! Music, Ludacris explains:

> [I]f strip clubs have any influence into what I do, it's only because Atlanta is the number-one strip club capital of the world. And basically, you know, we find ourselves going to strip clubs in Atlanta all the time. What people don't really understand about the strip clubs in Atlanta is that it's more of a club atmosphere than it is just going to see naked ladies. . . . [I]t's a place where so many music industry people come together and make a lot of business moves. You see a lot of artists and producers there. It's just almost like a networking facility, basically. You're going there to see Jermaine Dupri, or see L.A. Reid, because everyone is in there and it's just a lot of stars. You'd be surprised how many artists get on different songs just because they saw each other at a strip club in Atlanta, Georgia.

In Ludacris's hands, the strip club is rendered a more complex space. It takes on a male boardroom atmosphere where deals are brokered, video vixens scouted, invitations to appear on records are extended, and records are broken amid bodies undulating on poles, buttocks shaking furiously, and deep toe-touching bends.

* * *

Like Khia, whose regional hit "My Neck, My Back" was essentially "broke" in the strip clubs by dancers, hip hop mogul and Atlanta resident Dupri, whose latest video, "Gotta Getcha," featuring Janet Jackson and Nelly, is an ode to male voyeurism at strip clubs and peep shows, candidly admits in an October 2004 interview with *Vibe*: "I test all my records in the strip club. . . . If the girls really like to dance off one of your records, nine times out of 10, it's gon' be a hit record." In a VH1 documentary on Janet Jackson, producer Jimmy Jam revealed that street corner urban music stores used to be the street-level source for testing and breaking records in urban communities. If a song was blaring from the store, a hit was generally assured. As with so many other facets of hip hop culture that have challenged and altered both the recording industry and listeners' and viewers' tastes, the litmus test of a hip hop record's probability for success is now also tied to predominantly black strip clubs—in effect, pornographic black female labor. Like hip hop videos, the "hotness" of which is often measured by the amount of female flesh (predominantly black) and provocation offered—thus heavy rotation and an artist's breakout—the number of spins at a club and the dancers' responses are predictors of marketability.

Less costly than radio promotions, a mere five- to twenty-dollar club admission fee and a tip out to the DJ can assure at the very least a hearing among the most discerning of dancers. Strip clubs are to hip hop what Zogby (polling) is to politics—an indicator of what moves the crowd. The pole-swinging acrobatics, booty droppin', and p-poppin' are just as eagerly anticipated by networking artists and moguls for the sexual titillation offered as for a surety of a record's potential debut and rotation on *Billboard, 106 & Park*, MTV, and VH1. The sex work of dancers in strip clubs is moved to the veritable hip hop marketplace. Power moves and bottom lines have become decisively wedded to a booty clap.

The celebration of strip club culture, booty music, and the oft-bandied about moniker "Dirty South" in hip hop began in the South in the late 1980s and early 1990s. Acts like 2 Live Crew with their strip club friendly ditties helped set the stage for crunk, a southern offshoot of hip hop, which has fused strip club culture with hip hop to create what some critics dubiously refer to as "strip-hop." As hip hop elbowed its way into the mainstream, butt- and crotch-focused documentary films like *Shake Dance* (2002) and the Method Man–directed *The Strip Game* (2005), the hip hop infused *Strip Joint* magazine, and artists like the Ying Yang Twins of the *Billboard* chart–topping strip club warble "Wait (The Whisper Song)," T-Pain's "I'm N Luv (wit a Stripper)," and Lil' Jon have focused our collective attention more than ever on strip clubs.

It is not that pop culture and strip clubs have been hitherto strange bedfellows. Rock bands and their music, from Mötley Crüe's "Girls, Girls, Girls" to Nine Inch Nails's "Closer" (a perennial favorite at the Gold Club with the line "I want to fuck you like an animal"), have also famously frequented and had their hearings on the strip club scene. Their songs too permeated American households. That Nine Inch Nails's Trent Reznor would suggest in an April 1995 interview with Chris Heath, "I think my next album is going to be called 'Music for Titty Bars'" makes plain this not-so-odd coupling. But the primary listening audiences for these strip club ditties were whites. The global takeover of hip hop and its race-transcending commercial marketability appeals to a more highly diverse audience demographic.

As hip hop has taken over American popular culture,

strip clubs too have gone mainstream. An article in *USA Today* ballyhooed that "stripping . . . is now strutting into the mainstream, propelled by pop culture and the loosening of societal taboos."[3] Black women actresses too have played their fair share of strippers in popular mainstream movies like *Flashdance,* starring the ethnically ambiguous Jennifer Beals, *Independence Day* with Vivica A. Fox, and Halle Berry in *The Last Boy Scout.* Lela Rochon co-starred with the late Tupac Shakur in *Gang-Related,* while Gabrielle Union did a strip tease in the DMX-vehicle *Cradle to the Grave.* From Lisa Raye's breakout role in *The Player's Club* to Paula Jai Parker's fiery Lexus in *Hustle & Flow* to the 2005 BET Awards with Destiny's Child simulating a lap dance and young black girls "get(ting) low" at local talent shows in Nashville, women working in the strip trade have undeniably impacted (whether viewed negatively or positively) pop culture and gender politics in an unprecedented way. As D-Roc, the other half of the Ying Yang pair appreciatively remarked, "We've always been in every strip club in the United States, period. . . . Now, they inviting our strip-club music [thus the strip clubs and its gender dynamics] into they [*sic*] homes. You put it together, and you got a nice little chemistry there."[4] Indeed, we are living in an era of "stripper chic" as indicated by the popularity of Carmen Electra's *Aerobic Striptease* (2003), a series of striptease and lap dance aerobic workouts, entering the mainstream fitness fray. And ingénues like "White Chocolate," the half-Sicilian, half-black dancer in rapper Nelly's "Tip Drill," have left indelible visual instructions for, among other things, the uses of buttocks and credit cards.

In further exploring the intricacies of the new black gender politics, understanding the complex space of strip clubs and its culture is central. Not only because there has been an explosion, popularization, and mainstreaming of strip clubs since the 1990s, not only because hip hop generation black men frequent them in unprecedented numbers, and not only because more hip hop generation black women seek employment in them, but also because the purely transactional nature of the relationships in strip clubs (sexual fantasy for money) run parallel to gendered relations outside the clubs, that is, in hip hop generationers' intimate relationships. Hip hop generation men and women, at least in Atlanta and Las Vegas, also see strip clubs as a space for dating and stimulating nightlife entertainment; not surprisingly, the strip club then provides a model for interpersonal relationships. While many men may view bringing dates to strip clubs as the equivalent of bringing a sandwich to a picnic, we must acknowledge that they are not alone: many heterosexual single and married women want to go "where the boys are." They also want to vicariously experience the male freedom that the unselfconsciously nude, money-maker-shaking women exploit. As articles in *USA Today* and *The Las Vegas Sun* further suggest: "It has become trendy for *couples* and *women* to come."[5]

As discussed earlier, the Motivational Educational Entertainment study, *This Is My Reality,* noted the increasingly transactional nature of sex between urban, poor, hip hop generationers between the ages of thirteen and twenty. Teenagers and younger adults clearly are not alone here. All relationships, of course, are at the most basic levels mediated by transactions and negotiations. But with more than a little help from mainstream media, the transactional nature of relationships between hip hop generation men and women is now more than ever blatantly, undeniably, and unapologetically tied to sex for money and/or material goods. According to the study:

> [S]ex is something to be used and bartered with to get the right kind of car or clothes or be seen in the right places with the right people. . . . Urban youth, bigger consumers of television, music videos and movies than any other demographic group, are exposed to negative, conflicting and often destructive messages about sex and sexuality at alarming levels. . . . With their explicitly sexual lyrics and booty-shaking choreography, rap and hip hop artists have taken the battle of the sexes to a whole new level.[6]

The confluence of hip hop and strip club cultures then begs for closer scrutiny. Just how do race, gender, sexuality, and power operate in the strip trade? What are the experiences of hip hop generation women in the strip trade? How has hip hop provided a space for those experiences to be articulated? And what could those experiences tell us about hip hop generation gender politics?

*   *   *

The online *Strip Club Directory* and the *Exotic Dancer Directory* (renamed *The Adult Nightclubs Guide*), the Bibles of eye-candy enthusiasts and the go-to guides for women interested in performing in the adult entertainment industry, respectively, list over three thousand legal clubs worldwide and over two thousand nude and topless clubs in the United

States as of their 2006–2007 listings. However, the industry's trade association in America, ACE National (Association of Club Executives National), puts that club figure at over thirty-eight hundred with employees exceeding over five hundred thousand people. BlackExoticDancers.com/black stripclubs lists 210 predominantly black clubs—that is clubs whose dancers are 90 percent black and Latina.

In a study published by the Woodhull Freedom Foundation, Angelina Spencer, owner of the Penthouse Club in Cleveland, Ohio, and executive director of ACE National, notes:

> In America, there is no business like "show it all business." Economic downturn or not, there is one market that remains strong and sees regular growth year after year. . . . the "gentlemen's club" industry earns a respectable $15 billion share of the $75 billion global adult entertainment market.[7]

We shouldn't, however, be totally taken aback. America has long hungered for the sexually provocative; the only change has been the form such titillation has taken. We can see the roots of the stripping industry in burlesque, which began in the American theater in the 1840s. Sexual double entendres and scantily clad women would come to largely define the genre by the 1920s.[8] Though men like the female-impersonating Milton Berle also performed burlesque, women performing slow striptease to a state of undress with a comic shtick were the hallmark of burlesque entertainment in America. Performers like Gyspy Rose Lee, Little Egpyt with her bellydance (then considered scandalously provocative) and Lili St. Cyr rose to stardom as club owners looked for a way to bring in the crowds as live-theater attendance declined. Thus, g-strings and pasties were incorporated into costuming to avoid indecency laws as well as to titillate. A combination of raw comedy, sex play, choreography, and bump-and-grind music, old-style burlesque shows spoofed classics like *Ben Hur* with ribald theatrics and saucy titles such as *Bend Her.*

By the 1960s, old-style burlesque had practically vanished, but today, neo-burlesque is a thriving counter-cultural movement in an era rife with booty clapping and lap dancing. Troupes like the Harlem Shake Burlesque and shows organized by owner Katy K of Nashville, Tennessee's Katy K Ranch Dressing in the trendy 12th South neighborhood are part of the burlesque revival.

This revival, however, has been far outpaced by the booming growth of the adult entertainment industry. Strip clubs, go-go bars, shake bars, and gentlemen's clubs have been rapidly expanding in the United States since the 1990s. Part of this explosion is due to the trends of upscaling and mainstreaming. Middle-aged white (married) men have generally been the primary patrons of sex shows, peep shows, and the like. Demographic shifts have moved strip clubs from the dark, sleazy back-alley fringes to Main Street, USA. The launch of sex magnate Larry Flynt's Hustler Gentlemen's Clubs as compared to his 1970s raunchy working-class road house style clubs signals this trend.

At the same time, stripping has become a routine source of nightlife entertainment for an ever-increasing cross-section of American men (and women). Upscaling has had the effect of transforming strip clubs into clean and safe havens for sexual activities without sexual contact (in principle), particularly as fears about sexually transmitted diseases and the HIV/AIDS epidemic spread in the mid-1980s. Strip clubs are now viewed as a safer outlet for sex than prostitution—a criminalized sexual activity that was once closely associated with clubs. As a result of these new realities then, stripping no longer carries the social opprobrium it once did.

Stripping, it seems, is now nearly commonplace in American culture, as it has successfully reinvented itself through marketing and the blurring of the mainstream's once clear-cut boundaries of propriety. Sociologist Kate Hausbeck, who has studied the adult entertainment industry and stripping from her privileged vantage point as a professor at the University of Nevada at Las Vegas, relates in an interview on Minnesota Public Radio that strip clubs are becoming as common as fast food restaurants. As Hausbeck suggests, "When you watch Britney Spears in some of her videos . . . it's not terribly different than some of the performances you'd see in strip clubs . . . the kind of sexuality that's just so blatantly open."[9] The Mickey Mouse Club–turned–Strip Club antics of Spears and her pop culture counterpart Christina Aguilera are also mulled over by Lily Burana, former dancer, organizer of a union for dancers at Mitchell Brothers O'Farrell Theater in San Francisco, and feminist author of the memoir *Strip City*: "Your average teen star could go right on a strip stage without changing clothes."[10]

Feminism has also played its role. On the one hand, the spike in this form of sex tourism for American men can be viewed as a negative response to more women entering the workforce and changing gender roles in the family and in dating rituals. The sex-positive feminism of the late 1980s as embodied by crossover entertainment icons like Madonna and do-me feminist darling and patron saint of 1990s strippers Camille Paglia certainly contributed to the lessening of stripping's stigma for women, predominantly white women. Burana observes, "[F]eminism took a switch. It was no longer women saying, 'To be taken seriously, I need to be asexual.' Sexuality became more egalitarian."[11]

White women were not alone in their redefinition of the ways that the body could be used. Young black women have been keenly aware of the sea change in sexuality; it would be almost impossible, similarly, to ignore the glorification of strip clubs, so abundant in hip hop music, videos, movies, and CD covers. As former 2 Live Crew frontman, Uncle Luke relates,

> Right here on South Beach, before [hip hop] you would've seen black girls coming in from the ocean and they wouldn't have a bikini on. They'd have a towel all wrapped around them. Traditionally black people are really conservative. They're more conservative than conservative whites are, in my opinion. . . . With this whole tradition of sexuality [in hip hop] most black people are nervous about that.[12]

As we shall see, such developments in hip hop culture have made exotic dancing an acceptable, lucrative, and even empowering employment opportunity. Both the blurring of the lines between hip hop culture and strip culture and the pervasiveness of strip culture in hip hop encourages and redefines the profession as acceptable in the same way that hip hop embraced and attempted to redefine "nigger" (*niggaz, niggas*) and complicate the word "bitch" (*beotch, beeyatch,* and its magnanimous extension by men to men). For Anna (not her real name), a veteran dancer of four years who works at the popular Pink Slip in Brooklyn, Illinois, a nude hotspot for local (Chingy) and visiting (T.I.) rap artists and black men from all walks of life: "It's just entertainment. It's like going to the theater or a movie. Just spiced up."[13]

We should not, however, believe that stripping is now free of stigma. Even those hip hop celebrities who have done their stints in strip clubs like rapper-actor Eve or the "Black Marilyn Monroe," sex siren Trina, offer almost apologetic stories of errant youthful folly that portray good, short-term, hardworking versus evil, fast and easy money, sex-peddling dichotomies when speaking of themselves and the strip trade. As Miami rapper Trina relates:

> It was a topless bar. . . . I danced that night and I had like a thousand dollars. It was really an ego thing. . . . I was like, "I'mma [*sic*] take this money and I'm gonna pay for my real estate school." And I did it. The school was over the next month and I was still dancing. It's a form of evil temptation because you are so used to the money that you ain't thinking about yourself and what you want to become and how much more you can become.[14]

It is more than a teensy bit ironic that the exacting scrutiny Trina levels at stripping, selling sexual fantasy as a form of entertainment, is the very same scrutiny directed at punanny priestesses of hip hop like her. In later interviews, she does moderate her criticisms of stripping, relating that, "[I]t's almost like the same thing, because its just entertainment. You're both out hustling, trying to get money. . . . I feel like [stripping] should be something you do when you're trying to get your feet off the ground."[15] For women, stripping is still "a steel yourself and make that leap" over a yawning chasm, as Lily Burana makes clear. The current moment of stripper chic has not bridged the divide between "us," on the supposed side of propriety, and "them," those renegade women outside its boundaries. The trends of mainstreaming have also birthed a new archetypal stripper: one who shares our cutthroat ambitions to succeed, who entrepreneurially sells fantasies of herself. Yet, stigma persists.

The black exotic dancer faces judgment from not only the American culture at large, but also within the industry. As with so many industries being black comes with its own unique set of difficulties. The Exotic World Burlesque Museum and Strip Tease Hall of Fame, in California, off Route 66, offers one small example. The museum houses memorabilia and artifacts such as playbills, photographs, and costumes of the women who brought to life "the bump and grind Golden Age" (1900–1930) and beyond.

Josephine Baker, that high priestess of vaudeville and burlesque who made her topless and banana-skirt debut in 1926 in the Folies-Bergères in Paris, is fêted in the the Burlesque Hall of Fame. With the exceptions of Baker and the lesser-known Charletta Bates, the Hall of Fame offers very little else in the way of black women's contribution to burlesque. But there are of course numerous other black women who constitute a lost, but vital, component of burlesque. Given the de jure segregated racial politics in the United States, shimmying black women like the Harlem Shakers, a revue who performed burlesque in the 1950s, and countless other nameless performers, toiled primarily within the segregated worlds of black clubs or whites-only clubs that featured black performers, like the Cotton Club and Connie's Inn in Harlem during burlesque's golden era.

Integration, as in other aspects of American life, has superficially democratized and diversified strip clubs. But de facto segregation is still the principal modus operandi of the strip trade. Despite stripping's mainstream welcome, black women still find it difficult to earn the same money as their white dancer counterparts.[16] As former dancer Chris Bruckert writes in *Taking It Off, Putting It On: Women in the Strip Trade*:

> The most exclusive clubs accept only the most conventionally attractive strippers. Although managers are increasingly embracing a more complex consideration of beauty that values diversity, the standard continues to be the blond, tall, well-endowed beauty with tan lines and without visible tattoos. This idealized image of young white womanhood obviously has particular implications for women of colour.[17]

This may be slowly changing, though only on the surface. As in other facets of a consumer-capitalist-driven market, smart businesses recognize that diversity makes good business sense. Jacklyn "Diva" Bush relates that part of the success of the Gold Club was diversity: "Big breasts. A perky butt. Blond hair. Red hair. Tall. Short. Exotic. Kinky. Sweet. Any flavor girl a guy could possibly dream up, we had. Better than Baskin Robbins."[18] Like most other businesses in the United States, whether they are Fortune 500 or 100, or white-owned and operated, servicing (as in clientele) and employing (as in dancers) strip clubs, a smattering of women from racial and ethnic backgrounds other than white adds some variety to a club's dancer line-up. But as with other corporate strategies that are careful to avoid the tipping point where a white clientele would perceive a business as too black, white strip club managers and owners are also particularly mindful that too many black women might draw larger black patronage, marking a club as black, and thus inherently not upscale, and thus impacting bottom lines. Notwithstanding the fact that many black strip clubs advertise themselves as upscale, blackness in the strip trade industry connotes lower class, rawness, danger—a real walk on the wild side for the adventurous.

✳   ✳   ✳

Not surprisingly, race and beauty hierarchies also prevail in hip hop generation–frequented black clubs. The dancer-interviewees in *Shake Dance* noted how differently black men conducted themselves in predominantly white clubs and with the white women dancers who occasionally danced at black clubs like Magic City. As one dancer, Dawn "Camio" Brown, explained:

> Why do the black men feel like they can just let it all hang out and act ignorant in a black club? They will go to a white club, they act professional. . . . they talk about "the white man keeping the black man down," but you [black men] go to a white club and spend all your money in a white club and treat the white girls like "queens."

In response to Camio's frustration, Andra "Trouble" Williams continued:

> I know when I worked in a white club and I danced for black guys, they really act different when they are in a white club. They don't ask you to, "Bend over. Let me see it. Open it up.

Do this. Do that. . . ." I know at Magic City when our white girl gets on stage, brothers come from miles around, down the street, around the corner. They be like, "Damn!" Like she has something we don't have.

Magic City's management also practices their own version of diversity politics by employing a few white women in their dancer line-up, and, as it seems from Williams's description, at great profit. At play here, it seems, is the exoticization of whiteness and the specter of the forbidden-fruit syndrome. These women, in short, are put on a pedestal. Though they are also stigmatized because of the job, the behavior, respect, the "queenly" status conferred by black men upon white women who strip at black and white clubs seems vastly different than the experiences of black women at black clubs.

That black men take a certain license with black women at black clubs is clear from almost all the interviews with these dancers. The dancers find themselves treated as service merchandise, ordered to bend over and provide spread shots (glimpses of the vagina) while they shake and gyrate. Whether they police themselves or sense themselves to be under surveillance at predominantly white clubs, these same black men, it seems, also check their raunchiness at the door with both black and white dancers. And certainly Method Man and his entourage comported themselves more cautiously at the white clubs visited in the *Strip Game* documentary. After questioning black dancer after dancer about feminine hygiene and vaginal odor, upon entering a white establishment in Miami (Solid Gold), Method Man curses that, "Those white strippers think their pussies don't stink."

No questions about feminine hygiene are ventured though; and hands were sat upon, folded, or at their sides. Whether what lied between the white dancer's legs was foul smelling or not, these hip hop generation black men treated them in the way they perceived the white dancers perceived themselves: as "unfunky." What the white women had that the black women didn't was their whiteness and unfunkiness. The implied funkiness of black women dancing in black clubs then allows the men to "keep it real" and very street— "let it all hang out," as Camio suggested.

The mainstream strip trade favors not only an idealized youthful white femininity, but it also favors girl-next-door names like Jennifer, Kate, or Heidi, as opposed to the race- and (working-) class-laden names adopted by black women, like Alexus, Tiarra, Precious, or Ebony. In the end, white women who fit the ideal and even those who fall a bit short may fare better economically because they also have a broader array of employment opportunities (over three thousand legal clubs). Anna's one-week trial experience at Larry Flynt's Hustler Club in Washington Park, Illinois, confirms these dynamics:

> You have to work too hard at the [white clubs] for your money. Men who go to those clubs want to see white women. White men who come to black clubs come to see black women. I prefer working private parties and bachelor parties. You get your fees upfront; the tips are extra [money]. The white girls have cars and apartments. Their tricks [patrons] pay for all that. I want a hook-up like that.

The money to be made at clubs like the Pink Slip, Magic City, the now-defunct Gold Club, and Hustler is not on the stage floor where one dollar bills are ubiquitous and women must crawl around on all fours to gather them up, but with table dances, lap dances, and private dances, and in the VIP and champagne rooms. Women also work the private parties to supplement their income. Some dancers prefer the safety of clubs to private parties where the atmosphere has the potential to become a bit more raucous. The clientele at Hustler, an upscale nude club, attracts a predominantly white male crowd with more disposable income than the average male frequenting the Pink Slip. Thus many of the white dancers at Hustler were able to purchase cars and apartments from their work at the club. Indeed, dancers at upscale clubs can make upward of $100,000 annually.[19] Anna coveted the independence and material goods that the higher income allowed the white dancers, hence her reason for giving Hustler a whirl.

But Anna makes another point worthy of more consideration. Upscaling and mainstreaming has not altered the perception of stripping as not constituting "real work"—though it is, and hard work at that. While women may enter the exotic dancing profession relatively unskilled, women who continue certainly have to acquire more than rudimentary dancing skills in order to make money.

The cultivation of an outgoing personality, good conversational and listening skills, the physical demands of floor work and muscle strength needed to work the pole over the course of a four- to eight-hour shift, and the mental labor required to get into character in order to maximize earnings are especially onerous. As if these requirements aren't burdensome enough, the women expend a good deal of psychological labor in order to treat each patron as special in hopes of boosting earnings and cultivating potential regulars who can come to represent a dancer's bread and butter. There is also the tension that comes with fluctuating earnings not necessarily tied to the dancer's output but to the largesse of customers. And finally, and perhaps the most noteworthy, there are the endured insults and constant rejection (by customers) that can potentially undermine the supposedly sexually liberating aspects of stripping in which dancers imagine themselves as empowered, in control of male desire and their own sexuality.

Dancers are also importantly self-employed workers with no benefits or legally enforceable contracts. Since a portion of the dancer's earnings are paid out to the management (for the privilege of dancing at the club), the bartenders (for supplying overpriced drinks to customers and dancers), and the DJ (for maintaining the club atmosphere via music, hyping the dancers to potential clients, announcing house rules, such as "no touching," and plugging the VIP and champagne rooms which augment the dancer's earnings), where a dancer chooses (or is allowed) to work is often dependent on a club's house fees and payouts and whether those payouts are based on flat rates or percentages. The greater the earnings potential the more amenable a dancer is likely to be in terms of the payout structure.

At the Pink Slip, the fee to dance at the club per shift is twenty dollars: ten to management, five to the bar, and five to the DJ. Hustler is 30 percent of the dancer's earnings for the shift worked. Shaking her head in disgust, Anna relates: "I made $475 one night [at Hustler]. They wanted

30 percent. I was like, 'Hell no!' They told me I couldn't work there anymore. I was like fine. But I walked out of there with all my money. I don't like clubs where you work off percentages." Anna worked harder for "her money" at Hustler, earned less than the white dancers, and would have paid more in fees, a whopping $142, as opposed to the $20 fee at the Pink Slip. While the money to be made at strip clubs is accrued faster than at McDonald's where the minimum federal wage is $5.15 per hour, the work is much harder and the skills level much higher. All of these job factors combine to make the "easy" and "fast" money associated with stripping hard-earned. And the fallout from the stresses of stripping is varyingly described by Burana, Bush, and Anna as "stripper damage," "[turn]ing you out," having "an effect."[20] This fallout is usually compensated for with errant consumption.

Young black female strippers recognize that they are further marginalized by the fact that their occupation is regarded socially as on the cusp of sexual and moral propriety. Given the employment options in other low-skilled, marginalized, service-sector jobs, stripping pays better. Women strip for a number of reasons—they like to dance; they enjoy the attention and freedom from inhibitions about their bodies; they enjoy the power; but most strip for the money. As Anna insisted, "My other job pays the bills. I do this for extra money." The transactions in strip trade relationships provide men with outlets for their fantasies and women with money; but men are also paying the dancers to take a loss in social standing (the "ho stigma"); that money in turn is used in our capitalist-consumer-oriented culture to buy back that loss in standing—hence the stereotype of the status consumption lifestyle of strippers—through clothes, cars, and so forth. "Indulging," as Burana writes, "has as much appeal as investing."[21] And Karrine Steffans during her strip club days indulged more than she invested, ending up homeless and living with her son in her car, while Bush, who bought Prada for herself and all things Barbie for her daughters, eventually lost her home, an apartment, and even her dog, Chanel. But of course, many dancers use that money to pay for school, for transition to another life beyond the strip club, as Anna said she was doing; she was saving for her three daughters' education.

Strip clubs are not only racially stratified in terms of clientele and dancers but are also class-ridden sex tourism sites. Race, gender, and class collide in the sex entertainment industry in ways that find the vast majority of black women, mostly poor and working class like Anna, working in clubs where payouts are lower, the payoff is lower, and extras (the industry lingo for "extra-sexual" activities) are aggressively sought in the clubs and at private parties. Indeed, the alleged March 2006 racially motivated gang rape by white members of Duke University's lacrosse team of a young black coed and single mother of two from North Carolina Central University who danced because of the strip trade's promise of flexible hours and money attests to the pursuit of these extra-sexual activities, the extra legal lengths some will go to procure them, and the perceived legal repercussions to be meted out because of the woman's status as a stripper and a black female.

* * *

> The girls on us so derrty who you rollin wit'
> From Magic City to The Pink Slip in the Lou
> Them chicks love the diamonds that I get from Rob Jewels
> —Chingy, "Balla Baby," *Powerballin'*

The mention of the Pink Slip elicits a range of reactions. From a middle-aged, college-educated, business-owning, married father of two who has patronized the club: "Raunchy." From a young, stylish black woman who has frequented Nelly's "White Parties" at Plush Night Club in St. Louis: "Ghetto." From a thirty-something corporate type: a smile and a story about a male friend's preferring the Slip's realness to Hustler's Pledge-like polish on sex. From a regular guest at Missouri's various correctional facilities: "Thunder cats, Rappers," and words of caution, "Its rough. Go during the day." And from my father and stepmother: chuckles and more stories, which led me to believe that the Pink Slip's notoriety and offerings had indeed greatly impacted its across-the-water neighbors—St. Louis—regardless of class.

The Pink Slip is located off a rural highway in Brooklyn, Illinois, in a complex of flesh-peddling storefronts. Despite its Brooklyn, Illinois, location, everything east of St. Louis is simply referred to as the Eastside, as in east of St. Louis. Many St. Louisans cringe or bellow when those unfamiliar with the topography confuse St. Louis's Missouri location with the impoverished east of the Mississippi river city in Illinois. The dire poverty and disparities of East St. Louis provided the fodder for Jonathan Kozol's *Savage Inequalities: Children in America's Schools,* a definitive text on unequal access to quality education for our nation's black and poor. Ironically, even *Publisher's Weekly*'s review of Kozol's book situates East St. Louis in Missouri (which was probably much to the dismay of the St. Louis Superintendent of Schools).

From its one-level white cinder block façade, an aura of stab and jab admittedly wafts from the club. During my first in a series of visits to the club, the metal detectors at the entrance certainly gave me pause. And Anna, one of the dancers, would call the family-run operation, "The gutter, gutter, gutter." Notwithstanding the cesspool descriptor, the club is one of a few black strip clubs that is black-owned and operated and caters to a predominantly black clientele, though the white male construction-worker sitting at "perv row,"[22] mere inches away from a dancer's gyrating buttocks, was not the least bit troubled by these demographics. Just as I glided through the detectors, followed by my male companion, one of the manager's joked with a twenty-something black man behind me that his "wifey" (one of dancers to whom he had obviously taken a fancy) wasn't dancing today.

The club was much larger than it appeared from the outside. It had three stages—a main stage that was positioned in front of the DJ booth but at some distance; the other stages were off to the sides. Mirrors were strategically positioned on the walls closer to these stages. The lighting in the club was deliberately muted. Around the various stages were chair and table setups. The bar was off to the left-hand side. The club's VIP area with couches and a sports bar of sorts were concealed behind the bar's mirrors. Every inch of the club was used to maximize the customer's visual access to the dancers. The ridiculously low cover charge ($3 during the day, $5 at night) and the lack of a dress code assured a packed club. The bar, with absurdly pricey drinks and a two-drink minimum, did brisk sales even on slower day shifts. The busiest and most raucous days at the club were Thursday through Saturday evenings when the club had a mix of younger and older clientele, with the younger far outnumbering the older. The club had a steady stream of business during the day with college students, older men, married men who preferred the discretion offered by daytime visits, and businessmen for lunch and after-work drinks.

At any given time during the day shift, which began at noon when the club opened, there were roughly eight to ten dancers working. While one dancer immediately smiled at me when I entered the club, only Anna, who was unselfconsciously bare breasted, was bold enough to approach the bar. She was friendly and informed us that many of the women were not yet comfortable with the idea of couples. Despite male fantasies of ménage à trois, dancing for couples, or single women, implied that you were lesbian. Lesbiphobia was clearly at play; but lesbianism, as perceived by some of the "straight" dancers, could also have a direct impact on earnings. For them, the illusion of the dancer's availability to men would be ironically stripped away. They feared that they would be thought of as especially "freaky," and therefore subjected to heightened untoward male advances. Strip clubs, notwithstanding the fact that women are the main attractions and are charged with managing the space and boundaries, are decidedly male-centered erotic spaces. When it became clear that we were not potential "tricks," but that I was interested in black women who worked in the strip trade as part of a project, Anna settled into an easy conversation, answering my questions forthrightly as management moved about and the other dancers looked on in curiosity.

Between stories of petty rivalries, stolen wardrobes, accusations of poaching someone's "trick," drug and alcohol use by dancers to self-medicate or loosen inhibitions, and covert prostitution, she revealed that she preferred working the afternoon shift with its preponderance of mature, discreet, and oftentimes married men as opposed to the "disrespectful" younger men who frequented the club during the evenings. She was a mother of three. She worked the evening shift at a "big box" retailer. The Slip was extra money. She liked to read, naming a few popular fiction titles.

While most dancers refer to male patrons as "marks," the adoption of the word "trick," a word usually relegated to sex-trade work, reveals some overlap, not in practice as a general rule, but certainly in theory, between the strip trade and prostitution. The "disrespect" Anna abhorred by the young black men was related to their lack of restraint and their attempts to treat the dancers like "ho's" and "tricks." The men assumed that because their bodies (or at least a look and a lap dance) were purchasable, that the women were sexually available. Jacklyn "Diva" Bush also wrote of this slippage among customers even at the high-end Gold Club:

> Most of the customers who came into the Gold Club came in for conversation, for a little attention, then the other ten percent were looking for a little action. . . . they get this thought that since this is a strip club their mind flips—no it's a whorehouse. They forget they're in an adult entertainment establishment and so they offer money for sex.[23]

Exotic dancers sell fantasies. A strip club dancer will be and say whatever you want—for a price. Indeed, the dancer's job is to figure out what it is the customer wants and sell it to him (or her). In some respects, she *is* the ultimate hustler, trickster, and performance artist as she finagles the interplay of female agency and faux passivity.

Though strip clubs are generally envisioned as places where men can go to unwind with no fear of female rejection or emotional investment, as the women are there uniquely to service them, the gendered dynamics in strip clubs are more intricate. The appropriation of "trick" and "tricking" from prostitute vernacular to refer to their predominantly male clientele is a psychologically protective gesture; it is an emotional enabler to stripping for the women. It allows simultaneously a deliberate swipe at those male-cherished concepts of manhood and masculinity and a counter to the "ho stigma" attached to stripping. To be tricked by the trickster is to be a mark, weak, in this case, having a weakness of and for flesh. And that weakness is exploited by women for money. The "pimp-ho" nexus shifts in the strip club. In principle, the prototypical male pimp is endowed with an uncanny ability to smooth talk women (ho's) into selling their bodies for his profit; he in turn offers protection. Moreover, the male pimp not only receives profits from his stable but oftentimes sex. In the culture of hip hop, the pimp is glorified as a player of many women, a stud who sexes and uses women emotionally and physically. In the strip club, men become "ho's" and the dancers become the "pimps," as they trick men out of the money they've labored for outside the club, using a combination of smooth talk and exploitation of male desire through fantasy. The men, pimped for their monies, receive ostensibly only the illusion of sex—indeed everything but.

*   *   *

As the strip club's gender dynamics bleed over into hip hop generationers' everyday lives, they present another knotty layer in black gender politics. Strip clubs have always been on the scene. That a younger generation of black men have the access, means, and desire to frequent them is a new phenomenon—one part tied to wealth generation in the United States, the other to our commodity culture in which the most intimate of interpersonal relationships is rendered artificial, public, and purchasable.

For young black women, the transactional nature of hip hop generation strip trade relationships offers an alternative model to the "more for women" power feminism deftly articulated in Naomi Wolf's 1993 manifesto, *Fire with Fire: The New Female Power and How to Use It.*[24] These seemingly empowering transactions appear to run roughshod over the privileged status of black masculinity. Women purposefully use what they have to get what they want—whether it be sex, money, or some combination thereof—in the same way that men use money for all and sundry deal brokering. Inside and outside the strip clubs, hip hop generation men are perceived as potential marks, tricks, and ho's by hip hop generation women—wanna-be players who can now be just as easily played, sexed, and shook down for money as long as the men are led to *believe* they can "hit it." Young women were once upon a time willing to give the "self-help-return-to-a-pre-feminist-era" counsels of Ellen Fein and Sherrie Schneider's *The Rules* a try in order to gain respect,

commitment, and hopefully marriage. From mundane telephone etiquette (don't call him and rarely return his calls
—Rule Five) to the intricacies of the mating/dating rituals,
The Rules dispense good old-fashioned "let the man take the
lead" (Rule Seventeen) advice. At the bottom, there is still a
battle of the sexes raging. But women are encouraged to return to coy and demure rules of engagement. This generation of women, perhaps a bit more mercenary, are also more
likely to have multiple sexual partners to complement their
multifaceted lives. They are practitioners of a swaggering
black female masculinity, hence not especially concerned
with such trifles—at least in the short run. They are the
"new niggaz."

That sexism and misogyny are the sources of this recur-
ring gender trouble is undeniable. Hip hop generation young
women and girls appear to be rummaging around a junk-
yard of race and gender stereotypes for alternatives to sys-
tematic practices and biases in media, in their communities,
and in their relationships, which have devalued them and
shorn to scraps their selfhood. Sex becomes an easy standby,
a helpmate in the search for power for those who feel legitimately disempowered.

More fascinating and disturbing still than hip hop generation men's motivations for frequenting strip clubs and the
attendant merger of consumer capitalism, pop culture, and
sex, along with young black women's own riffs on these new
genders scripts, is that hip hop's most sexist and misogynist
inclinations in music videos, on DVDs (*Shake Dance* and
The Strip Game), and CDs have provided the only forum
for hip hop generation black women's experiences in the sex

entertainment industry to be publicly debated, scrutinized, and endlessly parsed. Middle-class autobiographical strip narratives on the order of Lily Burana's *Strip City,* Elizabeth Eaves's *Bare: On Women, Dancing, Sex, and Power,* Diamond's *A Stripper's Tail: Confessions of a Las Vegas Stripper,* Lauri Lewin's *Naked Is the Best Disguise: My Life as a Stripper,* Lacey Lane's *Confessions of a Stripper: Tales from The VIP Room,* and Heidi Mattson's *Ivy League Stripper* certainly reveal the beauty, gender, and class hierarchies and racial demographics of clubs, the prevalence of covert prostitution, and, more importantly, black women's marginality in our understanding of the strip trade. The sheer number of books by white women, autobiographical and scholarly, on stripping as opposed to the southern containment and marginalization of Jacklyn "Diva" Bush's *The Gold Room to the Court Room*—to date the first black woman's insider's account of the inner workings of an exclusive gentlemen's club—highlight how hip hop generation black women's experiences in the strip trade can be glossed over and ignored by mainstream publishers and in popular culture. Whereas white women's strip trade tales are pitched as "why good girls from good families do nasty, naughty things" or as tales of sexual liberation that border on thong-feminist tracts, the glossing over of black women's strip narratives effectively renders such experiences pedestrian, mundane, and unmarketable. And yet, black women's bodies are ubiquitous— from strip clubs to porn to hip hop videos; they have been critical to popular culture's promulgation of "stripper chic," and indeed hip hop culture in its latest permutation. But black women's voices and stories are not being heard. And what those voices and stories have to say about the state of hip hop generation sexual politics is rendered inconsequential.

Operating perhaps with the assumption that there is no readership for such work, *The New York Times* bestselling debut of Karrine Steffans's *Confessions of a Video Vixen*, who stripped in between bedding hip hop stars, will hopefully disprove such erroneous bottom-line publishing theories. The experiences of Anna, Steffans, the women in the flawed *Shake Dance* and *The Strip Game* documentaries, and Bush present black women's lives and work in the strip trade as varied, highly paradoxical, and as worthy of telling as white women's. If for no other reason than because hip hop culture is literally "waist deep" in the strip trade, these interviews, memoirs, and documentaries tell us a great deal about the troubling gender-clotted state of hip hop generation relationships and the impact these issues can have on black women's lives inside and outside the sex work industry.

The rapid expansion and significant revenue generation of gentlemen's clubs domestically exposes plainly the persistent patriarchal desire for passive, sexually available women. Young women who are not involved in the strip trade are freighted with the "cater to you" expectations that are part and parcel of strip club culture. Women in the strip trade find that the illusions they sell are conflated with the practices of the sex trade industry. These male-centric ideas and expectations are nothing new. The melding of strip club culture with hip hop culture resuscitates these ideas and expectations with new life, meanings, and socio-cultural outlets; they inform part of the new gender politics. Young women's push back against these dated concepts informs the other part of the new gender politics. A reliably feminist resistance to such sexist expectations by young women joins in tension with the practice of black female masculinity where mimicry (of the worst of male behavior) and conformity (to the stereotypes of female sexuality) masquerade as women's liberation. Like hip hop culture's offering of sexual liberation and expressivity to young black women, the "new niggaz" pose is but a sow's ear. It is a perversion of freedom, as it draws its cache not from politics but from the wells patriarchy has left exclusively to women: sex and beauty. On the surface at least and perhaps individually, the ends, as the cliché goes, seem to justify the means—female power seems to be achieved. But sex and beauty as trade commodities are depreciating assets. And for young black women as a group what accrues are harrowing statistics on sexually transmitted infections (STI), unwanted pregnancy, elective abortion as birth control, poverty, and incarceration.

CODA

or a Few Last Words on Hip Hop and Feminism

> I myself have never been able to figure out precisely what feminism is. I only know that people call me a feminist whenever I express sentiments that differentiate me from a doormat.
> —ZADIE SMITH, *On Beauty*

𝕿his book has now come full circle. Where we began with a discussion of hip hop and feminism, it seems only appropriate to conclude where we began, namely by revisiting these polemics surrounding feminism—where it intersects and faces off with hip hop and how young black women dicker with them both. While race may still be the conundrum of American culture—how we talk about it or not—feminism and hip hop are our culture's lightning rods for criticism, America's whipping girl and boy on issues from sexuality to declining family values. They may make strange bedfellows. But bedmates they are.

Hip hop is an obvious land mine of contradictions that we as women painstakingly negotiate and renegotiate. From every angle covered in this book, the sexism and sexual exploitation prevalent in hip hop culture continues to be a needling source of annoyance, frustration, and resentment. Eighteen-year-old college freshmen Sela[1] related in our discussion of hip hop music and its by-product, the music video:

> Hip hop and sexuality go hand-in-hand now. Before it was just hip hop. Now it's hip hop and girls [video models] because you don't see women [rappers]. . . . When I think about rapping and the types of songs, I already know what the video is going to be like. It's all about videos because they wouldn't sell if they were just on the radio because their lyrics suck! They really suck! . . . With videos now you know what's coming up next and you want to turn the channel. But it catches you and you are just sitting there like, "I cannot believe this!"[2]

And Grace, her classmate at a small liberal arts college in New York, adds, "They are starting to glorify the 'pimp/ho.' They get Bishop Don 'Magic' Juan out of Chicago [and] bring him up in his lime-green gold and have him stand on stage with a diamond cup. I mean what is that?! The whole 'pimp/ho' thing is really disturbing." The Archbishop Don "Magic" Juan, a former street hustler and pimp in Chicago, has achieved cult-like status as the "original true player"[3] in hip hop. He is author of *Pimpnosis* and *From Pimpstick to the Pulpit* and has appeared in popular films *Starsky and Hutch, S.W.A.T., Old School,* and *American Pimp,* as well as in music videos such as 50 Cent's "P.I.M.P." and Nelly's "Pimp Juice." With a guest invitee list that rivals the BET, MTV, VH1, and Grammy music award shows, the Don "Magic" Juan annually hosts "The Player's Ball" in Chicago. The ball was featured in the HBO special *Pimps Up, Ho's Down.*

From the young women's perspective, hip hop culture with respect to gender and representation is abysmal. Despite the pimps up–ho's down ethos represented by the Bishop and vaunted in popular culture, hip hop remains socially viable and relevant, if for but a few "conscious" rappers. Twenty-one-year-old Lauryn, an aspiring law student, suggests:

> Hip hop has been definitely relevant. I don't know that it has been more political in my generation. It used to be more political; it used to be much more conscious. You have a strain of conscious rappers like Nas or Mos Def or Jurassic Five or Common. It [politically conscious rap] still exists, but because of capitalism it has become such a commercialized industry. The politics has been set aside for money-making.[4]

Though the politics have been tempered by money, hip hop is given a generational relevancy pass that is withheld from feminism. Indeed, feminism has much work to do. As stated in the book's introductory chapter, every socio-cultural and political phenomenon has its quasi-saints and wholesale sinners. And thus, staggering stereotypes of feminism abound: some due to various media and some kicked up in our very own backyards.

The media-promulgated 1968 image of bra-burning, supposedly man-hating women at the Miss America Pageant in Atlantic City has been seared into the minds of American women. Jennifer, a twenty-something college senior, spoke about her experiences in a women's studies course during her first year of college. She took the course because of her growing interest in issues relating to women and was told to "reject the penis."[5] In mock ruefulness, she explained, "I can't." Even black feminism seemed a risky prospect because of perceived indoctrination into, as Lauryn offered, "a militant-no-men-type" movement.

What feminism is and what feminists look like conformed to all and sundry stereotypes. That is, until the fashionably hip ("feminists are notoriously bad dressers, preferring Birkenstocks"), witty ("feminists are serious with quite dour personalities"), smart and professionally accomplished (this is to be expected given feminists' ambitious nature and singular focus on career), stunning ("feminists are not especially attractive, eschewing all things associated with beauty") Joan Morgan arrived on the scene with a memoir. Morgan seemed the perfect antidote to the sexist morass that has become hip hop and young black women's antifeminist resistance. Her *When Chickenheads Come Home to Roost: My Life as a Hip-Hop Feminist* embraces both the untidiness of feminism and hip hop, opening a third space called hip hop feminism, which has room for the sextuplets (Shawnna, Trina, Lil' Kim, Remy Ma, Jacki-O, Foxy Brown), *Bitch* magazine, and so forth. The melding of two seemingly disparate movements—one primarily cultural, the other political—produces, as Morgan suggests, "a feminism brave enough to fuck with the grays. . . . We need a feminism committed to 'keeping it real' . . . where truth is no longer black and white but subtle, intriguing shades of gray."[6]

The linking of hip hop and feminism not only represents the simultaneous generational relevancy of both, but has the effect of offering hip hop the much-needed progressive gender analysis it lacks and feminism the ground it is undeniably losing. While various political pundits, news organizations, and even twenty- and thirty-something women like those I spoke with have been sounding the death knell for feminism, the Canadian-published magazine *This* with its

2005 May–June article "Feminism for Sale" shouted it from the rafters. According to Joseph Heath and Andrew Potter, the authors of "Feminism for Sale: The Real Reason the Women's Movement Is Losing Momentum,"

> There is widespread concern that . . . much of the momentum has been lost. One area where this shows up is in the unbending refusal by many . . . women to identify as feminists. . . . [They] enjoy the benefits that were won in the hard-fought battles between the sexes, but won't concede that the war needed to be fought in the first place. So despite the easy self-confidence with which these women are taking over universities and preparing to dominate the job market in the coming decades, the old guard feels the *war isn't over* [Heath and Potter's emphasis]. . . . But what if these young women have legitimate concerns? When people say that they are not feminist, even though they believe that men and women should be equal, it implies within in their minds, feminism is something *other* than simply a belief in the fundamental equality of men and women. The question therefore becomes, what is this extra baggage that feminism has acquired?[7]

Fair question. But the truth of the matter is that feminism has not acquired extra baggage, at least none that cannot be readily checked. The continued framing of women's concerns as "battles of the sexes" and "wars" in media, however, does not appeal to women who are weary of battle. And as women, specifically young black women, who highly value media (television, telecommunications, Internet, and advertising) according to a consumer profile conducted by *The U.S. Multicultural Women Market,* such continued framing of feminism as antagonistic to men, as sex battles, or as gender wars is particularly uninspiring and uninviting. As much as we are a "keep it real" generation, we are also a quintessentially "no more drama" generation.

Though many of us have never engaged in protracted struggles for equality or have been faced with the kinds of disabling discrimination that has no legal recourse, we have mothers, grandmothers, aunts, and others who have. Since many hard-fought battles have been won, enough to not substantially interfere with our access to goods and services, we have come to feel it's high time that someone enjoy those benefits. Why not us? And further, since part of the battles and wars involve not just taking on racism and sexism at large, but more specifically continuing black male chauvinism in the face of the grimmest statistics about heterosexual dating and marriage patterns, escalating black male incarceration rates, the HIV/AIDS pandemic, and racial disparities in health care (namely prostate cancer prevention and detection), many of us have deduced that a commitment to feminism or any kind of social justice movement calls for way too much, as we like to say, "energy" and "negativity"— drama.

At the bottom, feminism is not widely understood as a movement to end sexism, racism, and/or male privilege, but as predominantly and unalterably white and as a move to unseat aspiring black men. For many feminism is the equivalent of kicking a black man while he is down, kneeing him in the groin to make him holler, "Uncle," when we know full well that that groin will more than likely be consumed by prostate cancer because of unequal access to health care.

Such daunting complexities propel arguments regarding feminism's generational relevance. Yet it is precisely the language of feminism and the political gains made by feminists that allowed young women like Kim Osorio and Michelle Joyce to pursue legal recourse for gender discrimination and sexual harassment during their tenure at *The Source* magazine—even if many, feminist and not, question whether the representation of women in *The Source* under Osorio's stewardship as editor-at-large helped foster the very environment that both women protested.

Rather than speak of mergers, I, like the organizers of the landmark 2005 "Hip Hop and Feminism" conference at the University of Chicago, merely call for continued critical dialogue where the sorting of issues about race and class disparities, gender inequalities and heterosexism, and consumer culture can occur. I am not convinced that feminism is not motivated by exacting self-examination and self-criticism. I am convinced that hip hop culture is only beginning in earnest this self-reflective process and feminism is crucial to working through some of those contradictions. Besides, given my past pick-up work, I think feminism mixes it up rather well with the grays. That women, some of them feminists, some not, challenge hip hop's rap mavens to dialogue about the sexist implications of their full-time work demonstrates an openness to various shades of gray that border on graphite. While I too concede that feminism must continue to grapple with the grays that challenge us as women, I am, by way of conclusion, not a hip hop feminist; I continue to be a bit weary of identifying myself with, in the words of social critic Mark Anthony Neal, "a dying musical genre."[8] I am however a feminist writer of the hip hop generation who recognizes that whatever we call ourselves—feminists, hip hop feminists, or not—hip hop intersects with gender in ways that have us women renegotiating and debating the veritable gray areas taken up in *Pimps Up, Ho's Down* involving female pleasure, an affirming sexuality, beauty, and women's labor.

NOTES

NOTES TO THE PROLOGUE

1. These dates are offered up in Bakari Kitwana's *The Hip-Hop Generation: Young Blacks and the Crisis in African-American Culture* (New York: Basic Books, 2002).

NOTES TO THE INTRODUCTION

1. Nielson Media Research, May 2004.

2. Bakari Kitwana's *The Hip-Hop Generation: Young Blacks and the Crisis in African-American Culture* (New York: Basic Books, 2002); also see Kitwana's discussion of the "millennium generation" in *Why White Kids Love Hip-Hop* (New York: Basic Books, 2005). Also see Mark Anthony Neal's *Soul Babies: Black Popular Culture and the Post-Soul Aesthetic* (New York: Routledge, 2002); and Joan Morgan's *When Chickenheads Come Home to Roost: My Life a a Hip-Hop Feminist* (New York: Simon and Schuster, 1998).

3. The first convention mapped out a course of political action for hip hop generationers that included a 5-Point National Hip-Hop Political Agenda.

4. Marc Anthony Neal, "Foreword" in *Open Mike: Reflections on Philosophy, Race, Sex, Culture and Religion* (New York: Basic Books, 2003), xiv.

5. "RIAA Consumer Profile 2003," Recording Industry Association of America.

6. See Charisse Jones and Kumea Shorter-Gooden, *Shifting: The Double Lives of Black Women in America* (New York: HarperCollins, 2003); Marita Golden, *Don't Play in the Sun: One Woman's Journey through the Color Complex* (New York: Doubleday, 2004).

7. *Vibe,* November 2003, 66.

8. Motivational Educational Entertainment, *This Is My Reality: The Price of Sex, An Inside Look at Black Urban Youth Sexuality and the Role of the Media,* 2005, 26–27.

9. Julia Beverly, "Trick Daddy interview with Julia Beverly," *Ozone,* November 2005, 50.

10. All citations from author's interview with filmmaker in 2005.

11. Erin Raber, "Hip-Hop Her: Women Take Over the Underground Scene," *Curve Magazine,* 10:5, August 2000, 20.

12. Joan Morgan, *When Chickenheads Come Home to Roost,* 58.

13. See McWhorter's "How Hip-Hop Holds Blacks Back," *City Journal,* Summer 2003.

NOTES TO CHAPTER 1

1. See Serge R. Denisoff, *Inside MTV* (New Brunswick, NJ: Rutgers University Press, 1988); and E. Ann Kaplan, *Rocking Around the Clock: Music Television, Postmodernism, and Consumer Culture* (New York: Methuen, 1987).

2. Greg Tate, "Nigs R Us, or How Blackfolk Became Fetish Objects," in *Everything But the Burden: What White People Are Taking from Black Culture* (New York: Broadway Books, 2003), 7.

3. It is no coincidence that I deliberately selected movies, directors, and films that seem to resonate with the thug/gangsta creed of top-shelf hip hop artists.

4. Johnnie L. Roberts, "Fine Tuning a New Act," *Newsweek,* February 7, 2005, 40.

5. All citations from author's interview with the filmmaker in 2005.

6. Daniel R. Coleridge, "Top Model's Yaya Stays Strong," *TV Guide Insider Online,* December 23, 2004.

7. Ruth La Ferla, "Generation E.A.: Ethnically Ambiguous" in Fashion & Style Section, *The New York Times,* December 28, 2003, 1.

8. Rob Marriott, *Vibe Hip-Hop Divas* (New York: Three Rivers Press, 2001), 134.

9. Ibid., 136.

10. Ibid., 136.

11. Charisse Jones, "Black Women Make 'Shifts' to Succeed," *USA Today,* January 2, 2004, A13. A recent study of wage earnings among college-educated women found however that black and Asian women outearn their similarly educated white female counterparts ($41,100, $43,700, and $37,800, respectively). Latino women with undergraduate degrees earned $37,600. College-educated black men ($45,000) earned less than white, Latino ($49,000), and Asian ($52,000) men. All minority men earned significantly less than white men, who took in $66,000. See *The Chronicle of Higher Education,* Section: Government & Politics, Volume 51:31, 2004, A22.

12. Target Market News, "The Buying Power of Black America," 2003.

13. Veronica MacDonald, "Ethnic Hair Care: Acquisitions Are Changing the Market, But When It Comes to Product Development, Moisturization Remains the Mantra," *Happi-Household & Personal Products Industry,* 39(4): 60(9), April 2002.

14. Allison Samuels with Mary Carmichael, "Smooth Operations," *Newsweek,* July 5, 2004, 48.

15. *The U.S. Multicultural Women Market,* July 2004.

16. Erica Kennedy, *Bling!* (New York: Miramax Books, 2004).

17. Telephone interview with Lewis in 2005.

18. Allison Samuels, "Time to Tell It Like It Is: Sisters Talk Frankly about Black Men and White Colleagues, Money, Beauty—and the Prospect of Having to Choose between Racial Disloyalty and Being Alone," *Newsweek,* March 3, 2003, 52.

19. Advertisement, *XXL,* June 2005, 121.

20. In Marshall Eakin's *Brazil: The Once and Future Country* (New York: St. Martin's, 1997), 136–37.

21. Julia Chapin, "Beauty and the Beach," *Condé Nast Traveler,* May 2005, http://www.concierge.com/cntraveler/articles/detail?articleId=6057.

22. Matt Barone, "Ja Rule: Rates the Hits," AllHipHop.com, October 2004.

23. Frantz Fanon, *The Wretched of the Earth* (New York: Grove, 1963), 153–54.

24. "Brazil Struggles to Curb Sex Tourism," BBC News World Edition, December 2, 2004.

25. Norman Boucher, "Is There a Doctor on the Set?" *Brown Alumni Magazine,* September–October 2004, 55.

26. Department of Commerce's Consumer Expenditure Survey, 2003 and 2004.

27. Peter Wagner, "Opening Doors to Bahia," *Brazzil Online Magazine,* in Enterprise and Culture Section, April 2004.

28. *ChgoBachelor31_4u,* "Dos & Don'ts," AfricanAmericanMen BrazilianWomen@groups.msn.com, April 10, 2005, 8:45 a.m.

29. *bgcaliber1,* "Marrying a Brazilian Woman and Bringing Her Back to the States," AfricanAmericanMenBrazilianWomen@groups.msn .com, March 14, 2005, 5:00 a.m.

30. Frantz Fanon, *Black Skin, White Masks* (New York: Grove, 1967), 177.

31. *frihazeleyes30067,* "I'd Like to Address Some Concerns," March 20, 2005, 9:24 p.m.

NOTES TO CHAPTER 2

1. See Mama Specific Productions, "Aishah Shahidah Simmons NO! Interview," http://www.msppress.com/afro_mama.html.

2. Wells also discussed the interracial sexual violence and lynching directed at black women; but for most, "southern horrors" has come to stand for white male–black female sexual violence and black male lynching.

3. Katie Roiphe, *The Morning After: Sex, Fear, and Feminism* (Boston: Little, Brown, 1994), 6.

4. National Crime Victimization Survey 2004. Sexual assault in the United States occurs every two and a half minutes.

5. Ibid.

6. See statistics from 1997 to 2002 from the U.S. Department of Justice, Bureau of Justice, National Crime Victimization Survey, and

the National Institute of Justice and Centers for Disease Control. Also see Rape, Abuse and Incest National Network archives (RAINN). For stats on white male rapists, see U.S. Department of Justice, Bureau of Justice Statistics, Sex Offences and Offenders, *An Analysis of Data on Rape and Sexual Assault,* 1997, 24, 25, 34.

7. Jon Carmanica, "Seductive," *XXL,* June 2005, 96.

8. Earl Simmons, also known as DMX, as told to Smokey D. Fontaine, *E.A.R.L.: The Autobiography of DMX* (New York: HarperCollins, 2003), 79–80. Simmons also relates his first sexual encounter, which was more akin to sexual predation by an older woman.

9. Robin D. G. Kelley, *Race Rebels: Culture, Politics, and the Black Working Class* (New York: Free Press, 1994), 218.

10. Miller-Young and I met at an Association for the Study of the Worldwide African Diaspora in Rio de Janeiro, Brazil, in October 2005 where she was presenting her work on black women in the porn industry and I was presenting a paper on beauty culture and African American men's sex tourism in Brazil.

11. Luther Campbell and John R. Miller, *As Nasty as They Wanna Be: The Uncensored Story of Luther Campbell of the 2 Live Crew* (Fort Lee, NJ: Barricade Books, 1992), 152–53, 157.

12. Ibid.

13. Kimberlé Crenshaw, "Beyond Racism and Misogyny: Black Feminism and 2 Live Crew," *Boston Review: A Political and Literary Forum* 16, December 1991, http://bostonreview.net/BR16.6/crenshaw.html.

14. Tupac Shakur, "Wonda Why They Call U Bitch," *All Eyez on Me,* 1996.

15. See Jim Derogatis, "R. Kelly Flouting His Foes," *Chicago Sun-Times,* October 1, 2004, 57, and Letter to Editor, "Sun-Times Not Telling All about Kelly Critic," *Chicago Sun-Times,* October 14, 2004, 56.

16. Mary Mitchell, "Underage Sex Is No Joke, Despite R. Kelly's Antics," *Chicago Sun-Times,* October 3, 2004, 14.

17. See http://www.riaa.org (the Recording Industry Association of America Web site).

18. See the cover of "*XXL* Presents Hip-Hop Soul Vol. 1," *XXL,* Spring 2004.

19. Cited from the article "Sisters Act," *The Village Voice,* July 25, 1995, 15.

20. Definition from U.S. Department of Justice and Office for Victims of Crime, Acts 1992, No. 617.

21. Saptosa Foster, "Behind the Walls," *XXL,* November 2004, 126.

22. According to East Baton Rouge Prosecutor Sue Bernie. See Marlene Naanes, "Rapper Mystikal Gets 6-Year Term: Musician Convicted of Sexual Battery," *Baton Rouge Advocate,* January 16, 2004, 1B, 2B; Marlene Naanes, "Mystikal's Sentencing Delayed over Objection of Video Viewing," *Baton Rouge Advocate,* December 4, 2003, 7A; Marlene Naanes, "Mystikal, Two Bodyguards Plead Guilty to Sex Charges," *Baton Rouge Advocate,* June 27, 2003, 1B, 2B.

23. CNN Entertainment News, January 16, 2004; also see Marlene Naanes, "Rapper Mystikal Gets 6-Year Term" and "Mystikal's Sentencing Delayed."

24. Marlene Naanes, "Rapper Mystikal Gets 6-Year Term."

25. Jamie Foster Brown, "Mystikal to Fans: I'll Be Alright," *Sister2Sister,* October 2003, 74.

26. Brown, "Mystikal," 74.

27. Nekesa Mumbi Moody, "Jailed Lil' Kim Casts Herself as Victim," *USA Today,* September 22, 2005, http://www.usatoday.com/life/people/2005-09-22-lil-kim_x.htm?csp=34.

28. See Nat Hentoff's "The Public Rape of Catharine MacKinnon," *The Village Voice,* January 4, 1994, 16–17.

29. Tanya Horeck, *Public Rape: Representing Violation in Fiction and Film* (New York: Routledge, 2004), 3–4.

30. Saptosa Foster, "Behind the Wall," *XXL,* November 2004, 126.

31. Letter of apology is part of *The State of Colorado v. Kobe Bean Bryant* trial documents.

32. See pages 42–43 of trial transcripts, *The State of Colorado v. Kobe Bean Bryant.*

33. Interview with filmmaker in spring 2005 in Nashville, Tennessee.

34. Clip from *Fallen Champ: The Untold Story of Mike Tyson,* NBC, February 12, 1993.

NOTES TO CHAPTER 3

1. See Karrine Steffans, *Confessions of a Video Vixen* (New York: Amistad, 2005); also see *XXL: Hip-Hop on a Higher Level,* January–February 2005.

2. Bebe Buell's *Rebel Heart: An American Rock and Roll Journey* was published in 2001 (New York: St. Martin's Griffin).

3. "Data Show Value of College Degree," *The Chronicle of Higher Education,* Section: Government & Politics, Volume 51:31, 2004, A22.

4. George Gmelch and Patricia San Antonio's "Groupies and American Baseball," *Journal of Sport and Social Issues,* 22:1, 1998, 32–45.

5. In Derrick Bell, *Faces at the Bottom of the Well: The Permanence of Racism* (New York: Basic Books, 1993), he argues that white racism is a permanent and necessary part of our society rather than an aberrant excrescence.

6. *Ozone Magazine Third Annual Sex Issue,* November 2005, 61.

7. The authors of "Groupies and American Baseball" argue a similar point.

8. 213, "Groupie Luv," *The Hard Way,* 2004.

9. Julia Beverly, "JB's 2¢," *Ozone,* February 2005, 11.

10. "Groupie Confessions, Volume 2," *Ozone,* December–January 2005, 13.

11. Interview with Julia Beverly at Africasgateway.com, January 4, 2005.

12. Reference to Elizabeth Maguire's interracial academic mystery novel, *Thinner, Blonder, Whiter* (New York: Carroll & Graf, 2002).

13. Telephone conversation with Des Barres in fall 2005.

14. Centers for Disease Control and Prevention (CDC), *HIV/AIDS among Women,* 2004; CDC, *HIV/AIDS among African Americans,* 2005.

15. Interview with Teresa Wilitz, "More Confessions of the Video Vixen," *Essence*, October 2005, 270.

16. Elizabeth Mendez Berry, "Love Hurts: Rap's Black Eye," *Vibe*, March 2005, 162–68.

17. Karrine Steffans, *Confessions of a Video Vixen*, 109–10.

18. Lola Ogunnaike, "Turning the Tables on Rap's Player List," *The New York Times*, July 3, 2005, 10.

19. "Groupie Confessions," *Ozone*, November 2004, 21.

20. "Internet Goin' Nuts," *Ozone*, August 2005, A11.

21. Michele Norris, "Washington, D.C., Battles AIDS Health Crisis," *All Things Considered*, February 7, 2006.

22. "Internet Goin' Nuts," A11.

23. "Groupie Confessions," 20–21.

24. Nelly has a scholarship fund called P.I.M.P.

25. "Groupie Confessions, Volume 6," *Ozone*, May 2005, 15.

26. Gmelch and San Antonio, "Groupies and American Baseball," 37–39.

27. Ibid., 35.

28. "Groupie Confessions, Volume 2," 13.

29. "Groupie Confessions, Volume 3," *Ozone*, February 2005, 13.

30. "Groupie Confessions," 20–21.

31. Ibid., 20.

32. "Groupie Confessions, Volume 7," *Ozone*, August 2005, 13.

33. "Groupie Confessions," 21.

34. Ibid., 20.

35. Naomi Wolf, *The Beauty Myth: How Images of Beauty Are Used Against Women* (New York: Anchor, 1992), 291.

36. "Groupie Confessions, Volume 2," 13.

37. Ibid., 13.

38. Motivational Educational Entertainment, *This Is My Reality: The Price of Sex, An Inside Look at Black Urban Youth Sexuality and the Role of the Media*, 2005, 26.

39. Ibid., 31.

40. Ibid., 31.

41. Meredith Davis, "Is AIDS Awareness a Paradox? Despite Pro-

grams, Record Numbers of Blacks Are Infected or Dead," *Black Enterprise,* June 2005, 46.

NOTES TO CHAPTER 4

1. Niki Turner, *Sister2Sister,* October 2002, 32.

2. Jacklyn "Diva" Bush, *The Gold Club: The Jacklyn "Diva" Bush Story, How I Went from the Gold Room to the Court Room* (Los Angeles: Milligan Books, 2003), 7.

3. Kitty Bean Yancey, "Stripping's New Side," *USA Today,* October 28, 2003, http://www.usatoday.com/life/2003-10-27-stripclubs_x.htm.

4. Jon Caramanica, "Seductive," *XXL,* June 2005, 100.

5. Yancey, "Stripping's New Side"; Abigail Goldman, "Strip Clubs Begin to See Other Benefits of Women," *Las Vegas Sun,* July 3, 2006, http://www.lasvegassun.com/sunbin/sories/sun/2006/Jul/03/56667054.html.

6. Motivational Educational Entertainment, *This Is My Reality: The Price of Sex, An Inside Look at Black Urban Youth Sexuality and the Role of Media,* 2005, 25, 39, 41.

7. Angelina Spencer, "The Erotic Economy," Woodhull Freedom Foundation and Federation, n.d., 1.

8. Robert Allen, *Horrible Prettiness: Burlesque and American Culture* (Chapel Hill: University of North Carolina Press, 1991); Alison Kibler, *Rank Ladies: Gender and Cultural Hierarchy in American Vaudeville* (Chapel Hill: University of North Carolina Press, 1999).

9. Dan Gunderson, "The Sex Industry Grows," Minnesota Public Radio, March 4, 2002.

10. Yancey, "Stripping's New Side."

11. Ibid.

12. Julia Beverly Interview with Uncle Luke, *Ozone,* July 2006, 89.

13. From author's interview with Anna at the Pink Slip in July 2005. All quotes attributed to Anna throughout this chapter are taken from these interviews.

14. Niki Turner, "From Sister to Sister: Trina: The 'Bad Girls,' Part I," *Sister2Sister,* October 2002, 22.

15. *Ozone Magazine Third Annual Sex Issue,* November 2005, 35.

16. Anna from the Pink Slip relates this information as well as other dancers I interviewed at Magic City and The Pink Slip. See also Chris Bruckert's *Taking It Off, Putting It On: Women in the Strip Trade* (Toronto: Women's Press, 2002) and the documentary films *Shake Dance* (2002) and *Strip Game* (2005).

17. Bruckert, *Taking It Off,* 33–34.

18. Bush, *The Gold Club,* 11.

19. See Lily Burana, *Strip City: A Stripper's Farewell Journey across America* (New York: Miramax Books, 2001); Elisabeth Eaves, *Bare: The Naked Truth about Stripping* (Emeryville, CA: Seal Press, 2004); and *Strip Trade* (2005).

20. Burana, *Strip City,* 219; Bush, *The Gold Club,* 62; July 2005 interview with Anna.

21. Burana, *Strip City,* 261.

22. Pervert's row is in the front of the main stage.

23. Bush, *The Gold Club,* 90.

24. Naomi Wolf, *Fire with Fire: The New Female Power and How to Use It* (New York: Ballantine Books, 1993), 138.

NOTES TO CHAPTER 5

1. The names of the college women interviewed have been changed.

2. Interview with the author, April 2004.

3. See the Archbishop's Web site: http://www.thebishop.us.

4. Interview with author, April 2004.

5. Interview with author, April 2004.

6. Joan Morgan, *When Chickenheads Come Home to Roost: My Life as a Hip-Hop Feminist* (New York: Simon and Schuster, 1998), 59, 62.

7. Joseph Heath and Andrew Potter, "Feminism for Sale," *This,* May–June 2005, 21.

8. Interview between Mark Anthony Neal and T. Denean Sharpley-Whiting, "Hip Hop Not Your Pop's Culture," *Duke Magazine* 92:4, July–August 2006, http://www.dukemagazine.duke.edu/dukemag/issues/070806/hiphop1.html.

INDEX

culinity, 144–145, 147; of black
men, xvi, 51; measure of in hip
hop culture, 89; prison culture
and, xvi
The Massacre (50 Cent), 24
Master P, 91
Mattson, Heidi, *Ivy League Strip-
per,* xii, 145
Mayo, Kierna, 20
MC Lyte, xvi
McClodden, Tiona, 16, 17–18, 26
McWhorter, John, 19
"Me So Horny" (2 Live Crew), 61
Media's influence on: hip hop gen-
eration, 111; young black
women, 153
Medusa, 16, 17
Melle Mel, 5
"The Message" (Grandmaster
Flash & the Furious Five), xvi
Method Man: behavior in white *vs.*
black strip clubs, 132–133; *Con-
fessions of a Video Vixen's* effect
on, 101–103; Steffans and, 101;
The Strip Game, 120; wife, 92
*Michael "Mystikal" Tyler v. The
State of Louisiana,* 58
*Mike Gerard Tyson v. The State of
Indiana,* 55
Millennium generation, 5
Miller-Young, Mireille, 61
The Miseducation of Lauryn Hill
(Hill), 6
Misogyny: hip hop culture, 58–59,
61, 66–67, 110, 111; in United
States, 89
Miss Info (DJ Minya Oh), 97
Miss Jones Show, 96–97, 101–102
Miss Money, 16
Missy Elliott, xvii, 18
Mitchell, Mary, 69–70, 71

Modeling profession: Afrocentric
appearance, 29; *America's Next
Top Model* (TV show), xi, 28–
29; author's involvement in, xi–
xiii; cultural antipathy toward,
xi; female models, xi–xii; models
appearing in music video DVDs,
26–27
Monie Love, xvi
Moore, Michael, *Bowling for
Columbine,* 56
Morgan, Joan, 19, 20, 152
Morgan, Marcyliena, 10
The Morning After (Roiphe), 55–
56, 57
Morrison, Toni, 10, 63, 64
Mos Def, 151
Motivational Educational Enter-
tainment: on hip hop's core audi-
ence, 19; "Reaching the Hip-
Hop Generation," xv; *This Is
My Reality,* 14, 60, 111–112,
122–123
Mötley Crüe, 120
MTV (Music Television): music
videos on, 25, 26, 28; record's
potential debut/rotation on, 119
The Multicultural Economy 2004
(Selig Center for Economic
Growth), 44
Murder Inc., 17
Music video DVDs: on BET, 25,
26, 28; commercial success of
hip hop, 150; consumption of
and behavior, 26–27; directors
of, 25–26; ideal of beauty in,
30, 37–39, 42; impact on gender
politics, 26–27; models appearing in, 26–27; on MTV, 25, 26,
28; popularity of cable television, 25; sales of, 25; sexual

ABOUT THE AUTHOR

T. Denean Sharpley-Whiting is a feminist writer and researcher. She was named by cultural critic and scholar Michael Eric Dyson as a "rising star among black public intellectuals." A graduate of Brown University, Sharpley-Whiting is Professor of African American and Diaspora Studies and French at Vanderbilt University where she also directs the Program in African American and Diaspora Studies and serves as Director of the W. T. Bandy Center for Baudelaire and Modern French Studies. She lectures widely in the United States, Europe, and Africa. Author of four books, she has also co-edited three volumes, including *The Black Feminist Reader.*